Content

FOLLOW ME

PASTOR STEVE ORSILLO

DEDICATION

I DEDICATE this book to my wife Vicki who lived with me through all the ups and downs of writing and editing. She inspired me with her faith and absolute commitment to follow Jesus. She is my best friend and partner through this life of being Christian.

To my children Nicole, Mark, Danielle and Anthony. My babies. The Lord gave you to me, to cause me to be a better man. You have inspired me by your hearts and your love. I am so proud of each of you!

Also, to all the beloved brothers and sisters who have shared in this journey with me, from those that helped me to that altar and those who led me from it. Those who have follow me as I followed Christ will be the very definition of the abundant life that I have had the privilege to receive in this life, as I answered the call of Jesus to "follow Me."

To the wonderful pastors and leaders at The Father's House who minister daily in the message of the Gospel, giving their lives away for the "sake of the Kingdom of God." They are Nicole and Louie Wallace, Geordie and Stefanie Mumby, Minette Seabird, Danny Harp, Andy Engler, Maria Chattilon and Kristen Miller. Together you are the very definition of unity in the body of Christ and you demonstrate love so very richly to those you minister to.

To all the interns and lay ministers of The Father's House, where would we be without your love for the Lord? As it is added to our mix we experience a very rich and wonderful ministry. Our lives would be the poorer without your partnership.

Chapter 1

FOLLOW ME

How DOES the Lord choose His disciples? Jesus practiced a very interesting recruiting policy. He walks up to fellas fishing or collecting taxes and He says *"follow Me"* and that is it. They either do or they don't.

Jesus walks up and instead of giving a list of reasons or performing a series of miracles He just says *"follow Me."*

Now the things that you must do to follow Him or at least the deal that these disciples understood was that they would leave everything. They would leave their jobs and homes, their families, including all their possessions. One guy who said that he would follow as soon as he could bury his father was told to *"let the dead bury the dead"* and *"follow Me"* now, not a year from now when the mourning process was over. The leaving of all possessions, the denying of themselves, this seems to have been understood by the disciples when they dropped their nets or walked away from their tax tables, just plain leaving their professions behind.

What probably was not learned until later was the rest of the story. The understanding of the cost.

I am pretty sure that these men did not understand the words "pick up your cross" as an invitation to go and get crucified. Though they later figured that out. If you jump to the end of the story you see them scattering and going back to fishing. At the crucifixion, they did get a true revelation of the words *"pick up your cross and follow me."* They actually see Jesus on the cross. That would scare any sane man. These men were not chosen because they were dumb. No, history has taught us that these men were the pick of the litter, the cream of the crop, the best of the best and better than the rest type of guys.

Their religion, which was their biggest liability to their ability to accept the teachings of Jesus, was also the reason they were qualified to be chosen. They were Jews and you had to be a Jew to be called.

There is some evidence that they were chosen for the qualities of their character. For instance, Jesus said to Nathanael *"behold an Isra- elite in whom is no deceit."* To which Nathanael asked *"how do you know me?"* Jesus told him that he saw him. Maybe he saw them all and in a way that does not mean with the eyes. You do not automati- cally see that a man has "no deceit" just because you see him under a tree. It reveals that Jesus saw more than we sometimes understand.

Now Nathanael was not called in the same way as some of the other guys. He did not get the "follow me" recruitment.

Nathanael was compelled by his friend Philip with the words, *"I have found He of whom Moses foretold."* When Israel refused to hear God's voice they said "you tell us Moses, tell us what He said." Moses was told by God that one day He would raise up a prophet that they would "listen to." This Nathanael (or Bartholomew as he is called in the lists of the apostles) must have been hoping to have another chance at hearing God's voice. So when Philip says that he found the guy that Moses had foretold, it may be that Nathanael was ready for the chance to hear God. When Nathanael saw Jesus he makes a statement of belief saying *"you are the One."* The One that Moses had told us was coming. The One that we (Israel) would "listen to."

Nathanael chose to follow Jesus because Jesus is the One. The One that God would send to make His voice known to man. The one that men would not be afraid of.

Many people want to believe that these apostles were called because they were not the incredible men that they became. But I believe the story of Nathanael says that at the very least he was a man compelled to follow Jesus because of the great quality of his own character.

Regardless of what Jesus saw in them or even if they knew that He chose them for their character, we get to see some of the true heros of their time and ours. Their character becomes evident as the story unfolds.

Maybe it may help some people to believe that the disciples were "not the sharpest knives in the drawer." Then you can get excited when you see them as the "chip off the old block" guys or the "get a piece of the rock" heros that they became. Then it will help us believe that we can be something also. They see that these men came to Jesus as potter's clay and left this world as examples of being "born again."

As time goes on we see the revelation of the truth that they were realizing. Like Peter answering the question from Jesus *"who do you say that I am"* with the statement *"you are the Christ the son of the living God."* Like Thomas, when he realizes that Jesus is going to Jerusalem to die saying, *"let us go and die with him"* (not now Thomas, but later you will get your chance). Then there was the day Jesus washed all of their feet and alluded to the idea that as the leaders of this new 'way' they would be required to be the servants of all.

We get to follow along as they learn to preach the kingdom, heal the sick, cast out demons, all for the purpose of learning to follow Jesus.

We see their mistakes and failures also as they walk on water and then sink. When they cannot heal or cast out demons. As storms scare them and they do not know what to do. When they say the wrong things and are told to *"get behind me Satan."* When they see a guy casting out demons in Jesus' name and one of them asked, *"should we call down fire from heaven on him?"* I can only imagine what went through their minds when Jesus refused to stone prostitutes and had lunch with tax collectors and sinners. Their lifetime of religious training must have been screaming at them.

What a wonderful time of miracles and being personally taught by this bigger than life Son of Man. This One that they left all for. Many days of walking and listening as they are with Christ in the school of life, some days they know that He is The One, some days they must ask "who is this man?" If it were me, these questions would both be asked on the same day as I waver and question. They make great statements of faith and have honorable intentions as they endure the process of becoming like Him.

They were fishermen, tax collectors, some say that Thomas was a builder, plus men from other backgrounds came to fill the class of twelve that were with Christ in His school of discipleship. Some may have not been the "sharpest knives in the drawer." Others seem to be men of "no guile," "first cabin," even "top drawer" kind of guys.

In every response and action that they took, when taken in the context of a first century Jewish man being pulled in every direction, even the question, "shall we call fire down from heaven to consume that man," was in my opinion an attempt to live their belief in Jesus' Father to the fullest of their ability. Sinking after walking on water, asking Jesus to save them from the storm, not understanding that they had the power to feed the five thousand with two fish and five loaves, plus many more, these were all attempts to practice and learn what Jesus was teaching.

If I want someone to follow Jesus the way that He said to follow Him, all I will have to do is get them to meet Him. When they see Him or feel Him, then the person that I bring will also decide that Jesus is The One.

It was clear that Jesus wanted them to be able to do what He was doing. When Jesus said that we who believe would do the things that He did and even greater things than these would we do, He was telling us that He wanted us to be like Him. It was another way to say "follow me," or imitate Me.

When the disciples were in the boat during a storm or there were five thousand people to feed, or a father asked for his boy to be delivered from evil spirits, it is clear that Jesus expected them to do something. Jesus even wondered why they were so slow to use their faith, instead of His.

We get to read along in the great example of the disciple's response to the statement "follow me."

We see them at the end of Jesus' personal teaching time with them as He is arrested and taken to the High Priest's house, where they denied they even knew him and scattered in the night.

What a horrible night followed by three days of gut wrenching sorrow that must have been. The character shaping, as the Master Potter put the finishing touches on them, squeezing them into the shape that is required. Then came the fires of the kiln, as they were fired in the heat of trials that I cannot imagine.

These are truly the dark nights of the soul that many have endured and I know that some of us can relate to. It is truly the end of all hope. We say things like "I will never be happy again," "I will never love again," even life changing words like "I will never trust or believe again." Many have said "I did that once," "I even gave years of my life to it," "I left everything and look where it got me."

I have been in these dark places and I can feel the disciple's hearts when I read about this. It does not matter that they saw miracles and heard the truth. The reality before them is that Jesus, the one that they believe had come to save all mankind and set Israel free, was being beaten and crucified. It was dark and from the record it was despairing, probably completely confusing as well, they were probably experiencing gut wrenching fear to go with the rest. They had seen how these men who were in power at that time, the ones who had arrested Jesus, could make a man suffer and it scared them.

I wonder how they felt about their decision to follow after that. It had felt like a choosing of great honor on so many occasions in the past three years but I wonder how they felt about it now. Every time a horse went by the door or because of the sound of loud heavy footfalls their hearts would probably begin to race and they might have wondered, "have they come to arrest me also?"

Revelations of truth and the witness of many miracles is probably not much comfort when fear and despair have seized your soul.

Consider Peter, told in advance that he would deny Jesus, not only deny but claim that he never even knew Him. Oh Peter objected, even saying that they would have to kill him. I choke up and cry every time that I think about his feelings. I can feel Peter's thoughts as he wonders, did Jesus know all along that I was such a coward? So unfaithful and weak. "Why did He choose me ?" "Did He need a weakling to make Himself look strong or did He give me the great honor of dying next to him and I blew it ?"

This must have been a very dark day for all of them. Then there's John who tells us the story of Jesus' trial as if he were an eyewitness. It is like he is in the High Priest's house. Many believe that he was, having access as the son of Zebedee to enter. Yet there is no record of him stepping forward to testify or object.

Then comes the beatings and the cross. Oh Jesus, where are those whom you have loved so well? Those who left everything to answer Your call to "follow Me." Have they scattered as the prophet said they would?

Then we look at the cross, they are there also, these ones who followed him. Some are at the foot of the cross. The one Jesus asked to adopt His mother was there. He is aware of their presence. Those who have left everything to love Him, they are there, even if at a great distance. Perhaps from the walls of the city their eyes are upon Him in whom they have put all of their trust. The One who told them to "pick up your cross and follow Me." His words were ringing in their ears on this day. There He is on His cross, if they are to follow maybe they would be next.

Jesus was the only one of them on a cross that day though. Then He prays *"Father forgive them for they know not what they do."* He shouts *"it is finished."* These ones who love Him might be saying, what is finished? Was this a plan? What the heck is going on here?

All at once things began to change. A storm, a voice from heaven.

Later on the priests are running around whispering that something has happened in the temple, something about the veil being torn.

I feel the disciple's confusion, they get together and wait. They try to be faithful, they try to remember. Yet it is clear, they don't know what to do. I have been there and been that confused, I feel their pain.

I must say, I don't think they understood that all of this was going to happen when He recruited them with the simple statement "follow Me," when they dropped their lives and began to imitate Him. This is probably not where they imagined the road would take them.

He told them to "*let the dead bury the dead*" and "*pick up their cross*" and leave all behind. But it did not sound like this when they first heard it. Jesus also told them that His Father would "honor them" and He would bring them with Him where He was going, though not right away. But these words were probably not on their minds at the time.

I think that sometimes confusion of this kind is the result of the fact that the Lord's thoughts are not our thoughts. The best cure for this confusion is the revealing of the "rest of the story," the rest of God's plan.

Chapter 2

THEN IT ALL CHANGES

SO HERE they are, confused as I said, probably asking "did He say something about the third day?" Never losing sight of the fact that they just saw Him brutally murdered. Never forgetting that He had gone to this sacrifice alone. Trying to remember the night He was arrested, what was He saying? Something about us staying awake with Him. Did anybody do that?

When the women went to the grave, they came back with a report that they saw Him, "He is alive." What news is this? Mary says that He told her to "*quickly now go tell my disciples, and Peter, that I have risen just as I said.*" Then two of the disciples ran to the grave. I cannot imagine the range of emotion as they try to arrange their thoughts. Could this possibly be true? Could He really be alive? Could He conquer death? He did it with Lazarus.

John arrives at the tomb first but Peter runs in, there is the empty grave and the linen unwrapped. When they see this, then they believed. He is risen.

Mary Magdalene saw Jesus outside the tomb and He said to her, "*Go tell my brothers,*" "*I am returning to my Father and your Father, to my God and your God.*" The 'disciple' title has changed to 'brother.' At a time when they think that they are the unfaithful followers Jesus is calling them His brothers, and His Father their Father. The truth is that "it is finished." The work of restoring man to God the Father and the act of conquering death has been finished. "*Oh death where is thy sting.*"

The meaning of the title 'His disciple' has been changed forever and it is the very essence and definition of the word Christian. It means being transformed into His image and likeness. Now the work has only begun for these heros of the faith. Now the "pick up your cross and follow me" and "no greater love" statements of Jesus have new meaning. Now, "laying down his life for his brother" was beginning to come clear to them as the answer to the question of what was expected when a man follows this Jesus.

I doubt that when Jesus walked up to them and said "follow me" they understood the wonder of what was going to happen next. He told them that they should wait until the Holy Spirit would come upon them. When this happened they would receive "power from on high."

Jesus was not calling them only to go where He goes, to step in His footsteps as the description of following Him. Jesus was actually telling them to "follow Him" in His identity. To live as Him on the earth. Heal like He healed, speak what He spoke, and more. Jesus came and gave any who would "follow Him" the power to know God and hear His voice. Jesus told Mary to tell them that His Father would be their Father. Even His sonship was theirs to be had by just answering Jesus' call to "follow Me."

The example we have in these men is that after "leaving all" they still had to learn from Him, they had to "listen to Him," as the Father told them, they would have to obey and be transformed, even changing their theology to accept this New Covenant with God. The process did not seem to be easy as we get to watch and read along as the story unfolds.

Chapter 3

WHERE I AM GOING YOU CANNOT GO, YET

JESUS HAS this talk with His disciples.

"Little children, I am with you a little while longer. You will seek Me; and as I said to the Jews, now I also say to you, Where I am going, you cannot come."

"A new commandment I give to you, that you love one another, even as I have loved you, that you also love one another. By this all men will know that you are My disciples, if you have love for one another. Simon Peter said to Him, Lord, where are You going? Jesus answered, Where I go, you cannot follow Me now; but you will follow later."

"Peter said to Him, Lord, why can I not follow You right now? I will lay down my life for You. Jesus answered, Will you lay down your life for Me? Truly, truly, I say to you, a rooster will not crow until you deny Me three times."

"Where I am going you cannot come." This statement seems to really confuse the disciples. They want to know what is going on here. We did not leave everything to follow you, only to be kicked to the curb now.

He had just washed their feet, revealed who would betray Him and said that to "receive Him was to receive the one who sent Him."

Then He drops the bomb on them. "Where I am going you cannot come." (Now that He has gone there and they have seen it, they might not want to go anyways), there really are crosses involved!

After the resurrection Jesus said, "*I am going to my Father and your Father.*" They might have said, "what, going again? He just got back, we are just thinking we know what is going on here and He says that He is leaving again."

About now, when the revelation of the future is on all of their minds, they ask "are you going to restore Israel now Jesus?" But He said, "I am going to my Father," and they remember that He said, "where I am going you cannot come."

They had believed in His Father all their lives. They had heard Him talk about His Father for three years now. They had heard the Father's voice call Jesus His Son from the sky at least three times, because of this He now has their attention.

He has just conquered death. Now they are listening closely and He does not disappoint. He says something so incredible to a 4 B.C. Jewish man that it is hard to believe that even one of them did not object to it. He said "*I will ask the Father, and He will give you another Helper, that He may be with you forever; that is the Spirit of truth, whom the world cannot receive, because it does not see Him or know Him, but you know Him because He abides with you and will be in you. I will not leave you as orphans; I will come to you.*"

Now 21st century Christians tend to take this for granted but to these men from this time, this was the miracle of all miracles. "*John baptizes you with water but I shall baptize you with the Holy Spirit,*" and "*You will receive power when the Holy Spirit comes upon you.*" Baptize, immerse, fill? With the Holy Spirit? Is this possible, can they believe it? They do believe it now. It all makes sense now what He had said *"My Father and I will make our Home in you."* I think that to me the indwelling Spirit of God is the most incredible miracle of mercy that I find in the Kingdom of The Father.

I have heard of people giving their lives for their friends. I have heard of people forgiving the most terrible wrongs and doctors heal people all the time. These, though fantastic have been done by others. This baptizing, immersing and filling with the Holy Spirit boggles the mind. The Holiness of God in the flesh of man, His righteousness and Holiness placed on me as a garment, causing me to be able to receive the baptism of the Holy Spirit, (He will be in you), to be the home of the Father and the Son, this is mind boggling.

Where I go Jesus goes, what I do Jesus does, my body is His home. I love my home, some days I cannot wait to get there and just relax, I love it. Jesus loves His home and His home is me.

In the Jordan river the Spirit landed on Jesus like a dove and the verse says that it "remained on Him." This is one thing He meant when He said "follow me." We would become like Him, the dwelling place of God's Spirit and that it would remain on us.

Jesus said *"You will be My witnesses to the ends of the earth."* The disciples may have been thinking something like this, the ends of the earth, where is that? We are Jewish men born and bred, we can't go to the ends of the earth unless you mean within reach of the temple so that we can make sacrifices.

A conversation amongst themselves might sound like this, 'Okay let's recap, there I was fishing and this incredible man comes to me and says " follow Me." It was as though I was in a fog. What was that presence around me? What did I do? I dropped my nets right there and then and just went. What was I thinking? What do I do now that Jesus is gone? I am going fishing, it is where I belong.

Just when their families think that these men have regained their senses, Jesus shows up and says things like, *"I will baptize you with the Holy Spirit." "When the Holy Spirit comes upon you, you will receive power. Go into all the world and make disciples. You will be*

My witnesses to the ends of the earth." They might be thinking, we laid our hands on the sick and we commanded demons-but the Holiness of God in the flesh of man? "Baptized in the Holy Spirit ?" Is this possible?

Again they also might be thinking 'the Holy Presence of God in the sinful body of man? Has not His Presence dwelt in The Ark of the Covenant behind the veil in the Holy of Holies, where sinful man could not be harmed by His wrath upon disobedience? Did He not tell Moses that on the day that Moses would see Him that he would surely die? How about the hemorrhoids of the Philistines, and the death of Uzza? The victories of Israel's armies all because of the presence of the Presence? God himself giving His name to Moses as the Present One?

Here Jesus is saying something so incredible, "you will be baptized with the Holy Spirit" and "power will come upon you." Jesus had said to them that they could *"ask whatsoever you will in My name and it will be done for you."*

Now He says, *"Where I go, you cannot follow Me now; but you will follow later."* Yes Lord I will follow you, and do the things that you have asked of me. I will be a home for the Spirit of Your Father. And yes, all men will know that I am Your disciple. What a promise! What a task! *"A new commandment I give to you, that you love one another, even as I have loved you, that you also love one another."* New commands, new life, new power and later I will go where He goes, to be with our Father. The disciples had become "born again" to new life, and to new purpose, to many promises of power, a new relationship with God. He would be their Father. They would have His name.

Chapter 4

ARMED WITH HIS NAME

WHEN JESUS was praying for His disciples and He said that *"My Father and I will make our home in you,"* they probably did not understand this at the time that He said it, then Jesus reveals another interesting thing when He said to the Father *"I have shown them your name."* I think He was saying that one very important attribute for a disciple is that a disciple knows what it means to know the name of the Father. Jesus was saying that He was successful in His ministry to the disciples because He had revealed the Father's name, not a common name like Bob but the name that reveals His nature like "Faithful one" or "Author and Finisher of our faith."

What difficulties could cause a man to walk away from "The Way, The Truth and The Life?" As Peter said "where would we go," when once we have been armed with the Name of the Father. Through so many hard times I have used the attributes of God as my shield and my helmet. He has been my breastplate. When it feels like I will perish for lack of His presence "The Living Water" has refreshed me.

If it seems like darkness has enveloped me then "The Light of the World" comes to show me the way. If hungry then "The Bread that came down from heaven." Sinking? He's "The Rock." Need to build a new vision for your life? The "Chief Cornerstone" would make a huge difference.

I don't believe that there is any situation that you could be in, that knowing the names of God would not arm you for victory. As I said, His name is not a common name like Bill or Bob, no, it is an attribute like "Faithful One."

Moses actually asked God what His name was and when God told him that it was "*I am that I am,*" Moses asked again because he had always been taught that gods have a name. Well this God was telling Moses to go back to the ruthless king that he just escaped from. God wanted Moses to tell Pharaoh to free all of his slaves and let them leave Egypt. Moses just wanted to be able to let the Pharaoh know who had sent him. God said "*tell him that I am that I am sent you.*" I would have been way more confused than Moses was because in English that does not make any sense, it just means tell him that I exist. The meaning of these words, seems to be that God's answer was "go tell them the One God who is present sent you." That not only makes sense but is probably the most powerful statement ever made in the presence of man. His name is that He is "The Present One," and what it meant to Moses and to us today is that He is present with us. When I personalize it, which is how it was intended, it is He is present with me. So Moses was to tell Pharaoh that God is with me and you will listen to Him in my voice. He is the God that you feel around you.

In Moses' time, in your time, continuing for all time, He is the One Who is present, when you gaze upon the natural wonders of the world like the oceans or the Grand Canyon, Yosemite Valley or just gaze at the stars. Whenever you have contact with the creation that makes you feel the wonder of it all, it is the residue of His presence that you feel. He was there in creation's powerful force. His act of creation has a signature of His presence. Just a few days ago I dangled my feet off of the edge of the Grand Canyon. What I felt was the awesome presence of the Creator of Heaven and Earth. People who don't believe try to explain what they feel by saying that this canyon eroded like this over millions and millions of years. I have seen erosion in my back yard and on construction sites and erosion does not feel like this. The residue of His presence and creation power does.

When you speak He hears you, when you act He sees you. The most important aspect of His name that He wants us to know is that He is present. "Emmanuel, God is with us," He has made His home in us.

He has called us to "follow Him," to imitate Him and be His presence on the earth. To love like He loved us, to give like He gave to us. We are armed with His name and He is the One who is present with us and in us.

Jesus said *"I have shown them your name,"* before the cross, before the resurrection morning. He said it before He promised the Baptizing of the Holy Spirit. I think it was Jesus' intention to give His disciples a revelation of the Father's name during their time of being with Him. He came to show them the Father. That is what He said. In His prayer Jesus was saying that the mission was accomplished. "I have shown them your name."

It is as if He had a check list during His ministry. Baptize them in the revelation of the Father, check. Baptize them in the power of faith, check. Baptize them in the cost of sin, someone has got to bleed, check. Conquer death, check. Take away their sins, check. Then the fulfillment of the Father's promise, the baptizing of the Holy Spirit. I believe this is the completion of the process that the Apostle described when he said that *"to those who believed in His name He gave the power to become the children of God."* They were disciples at this time. His resurrection was the next step to them becoming sons of God. By conquering death He purchased for them the right to become the Father's sons, the rest was up to them imitating Him. He came out of the grave and called them His brothers, His Father their Father. Then He told them not to go anywhere until the Holy Spirit came upon them. Again, no one would expect the Holy Spirit, the Father or the Son of God to be in them. This would be beyond their imagination to even believe, until it happened. After this the transformation could be complete. If they believe, then they can become sons.

I have read the rest of the story, it says that the disciples will continue to answer the call of Jesus to "follow Me" for the rest of their lives and live as sons to the Father of all creation, the Lord of Heaven and King over all of the earth. They will live lives that I can imitate and follow as well. They will write books and send letters that I call the Word of God and I will obey these words as the commands upon my life as a disciple. These men who have answered the call of Jesus to "follow Me" have become men who could say to others like me, "follow me and you will not get lost."

Chapter 5

PUT ON JESUS

IN ISAIAH chapter 59 the prophet says that wrong is right and right is wrong. Men who "turn aside from evil make themselves a prey." Then it says that God could not find anyone who would "intercede," and continues, *"then His own arm brought salvation to Him." "He put on righteousness like a breastplate and a helmet of salvation on His head, and wrapped Himself with zeal as a mantel"*

Paul the Apostle uses these words to give us the courage to go after our enemies with the message of salvation, being armed with the protection of God's name. Paul tells us that we should put on this armor to protect ourselves from the fiery darts of the enemy. The helmet of salvation and the breastplate of righteousness are the characteristics that Isaiah used to describe how God was going to restore salvation to His people. God took it in His own hands. If no-one else will do it right then you're gonna have to do it yourself.

Paul put on these pieces of armor and then he instructed us to put on these pieces of armor. If you read chapter 59 of Isaiah you will see that this is describing Jesus. You will find out that God has become a man and His redeemer has come to Zion.

Put on Jesus and you have put on the helmet of salvation, the breastplate of righteousness, plus you get the shield of faith. When you read Paul's instructions he tells you that you get even more, you get shoes and a sword, but wait there's more, infinitely more. These descriptions are the continuation of Jesus' statement that He has "shown forth His name to us." Jesus is the Helmet of my Salvation and the Breastplate of my Righteousness.

Jesus is the Armor of God. We must have put on Jesus for every action that we take. This makes us safe from our enemies. We are like armored tanks in spiritual warfare. If I have put on Jesus, I have put on salvation and righteousness. I have the truth and the word in my mouth becomes very dangerous to the bondages that enslave people and my faith protects me like a shield. No fiery darts even worry me, I have Jesus and He is Faith.

The next thing that happens is that I become a man who God can use, a man that God can call, a useful man. Simply put, one who will stand in the gap, protect the vineyard, remain in the day of trouble. This is not the job for a man that God has simply hired to work the vineyard. This is the act of a son, one who believes that this is his Father's vineyard and no one gets to rob it or pillage the bond servants who work for his Father.

The purpose of the armor is that we should stand firm and be strong. Paul was just trying to get us to put on Jesus as our confidence, that we need not live in fear. Our faith in Jesus would cause us to be invincible in the fight for Jesus' people and the purposes for which He endured the cross. He did not die in vain if I can only see that faith, salvation and righteousness are not a thing but a who. That something is not with me but someone is in me. Jesus in me is the Hope of the Kingdom and the fulfillment of the Father's purpose, His purpose that Jesus died on the cross for. If the King of Kings is in me then the Kingdom has come, His will, will be done here just as it is in Heaven. The King, who happens to be my Father has sent me in His name.

It is just me who will be deciding whether this is done. If I see them hungry and feed them they will get fed. If I see the storm and calm it, then the storm will get calmed. If I recognize that a demon is enslaving someone, they will be free if I free them. They will stay enslaved if I don't. If I see someone sick and lay hands on them they will recover. If I see someone sick and wish them be warm and well fed they probably will not recover. But they will probably be warm and well fed.

If we just leave it in God's hands, saying that I must be sick because it is God's will, He will heal me if He wants to, then I will probably stay sick. God always wanted us healed, He is our Father. I will be healed when I believe in faith (Jesus) that God will heal me and I see Him (Jesus) in a disciple who believes that Jesus in Him wants to heal me. God's will is constant, a disciple's anointing (Jesus in them) should be constant but isn't always, my faith sometimes doubts and sometimes gets scared maybe from seeing the storm. So, the healing that I need is mine if I find a disciple who believes in their anointing, an anointing which is automatic when they have been filled with the Holy Spirit and I believe that they can heal me. My faith (Jesus put on) in their anointing (Jesus in them) and God's will is done, I am healed. My testimony is that God has healed me by the cross of Jesus Christ. Yet nothing would have happened without Faith and anointing and one more thing, a disciple who took action. If I am hungry and the disciples that I come in contact with don't take action with their faith and they leave it up to God to feed me. I should at this time start looking for someone who will take action, someone who is an armored tank in the field of battle, someone that I can get behind. Someone that walks with God in faith, righteousness and an understanding of what being filled with the Holy Spirit is supposed to bring them. Someone who has put on Jesus. I look for a Son! If I do this I will be fed.

What would that look like? Would it look like Jesus, if you put on Jesus? Would the world be a safer place for the poor in spirit and the demon controlled people? Would it look like a bunch of Jesus' walking around? Wow !! Would that be something. One Jesus back in His day changed the face of the earth and affected man's culture for all time. What would two do? Or thousands? Twelve certainly did a lot of culture changing.

I know that these words just go over most people's heads, if they have not gone over yours, maybe you are ready to understand that the simple phrase "follow Me," means much more than to trace steps or walk in a direction. It means an imitation or reflection that is learned by first hearing, then imitating, the end being that we resemble and represent Jesus as imitators or replicas.

The word disciple means learner but it was not very long after the ascension of Jesus that disciples began to be called Christians. The people named them this because these men resembled the stories that they heard about Jesus. This happened as the Apostles told the stories of Jesus and repeated the teachings of Jesus, even writing them down for all to read. The people began to understand that these men were very much like Jesus. So they called them little Jesus' or Christians. If Jesus were the Anointed One then they were 'little anointed ones.' They were replicas in behavior and wisdom. They also demonstrated the power that Jesus had. Plus, they lived a righteous life in front of the people as an example of the Savior that they peached. Paul who was a first, second generation Apostle even taught that you change your behavior to live what others think is right so as to be able to preach the Gospel to them. Not compromising your standards of righteousness but in terms of traditions and ways of living so as not to detract from the message of hope in salvation.

So, what does a replica do? The Apostles were very good examples of the answer. We get to follow them in the book of Acts and through their epistles. History has been written by secular authors to let us know that they had a profound effect on their culture.

These men who left all to follow and made many mistakes went on to change the world. They found out that their faith was misguided and they did not know as much as they thought. They denied Him and received His forgiveness. One time in a boat they had been afraid of the storm so they woke Jesus up to ask for help. He rebuked them for their unbelief.

Now if I am in a storm and the Lord is with me, is it wrong to pray His deliverance or should I use the power and authority that He gave to me to calm the storm myself? They were learning and so am I. How do we learn if we never get ourselves into storms? They were afraid, Jesus was asleep. There is a lot to learn when we are somewhere between being deathly afraid and asleep. If He did it, then we can do it. As replicas or little anointed ones, we should seek the Son and seek to act as sons.

When people like you or me actually get this, you would think that we would be received like conquering heros. By the people seeking the Lord, we are! Yet by the ones whose power is being challenged, not so much. Also the people who lose money from it are not too happy either. Such as those who sell prayers like the Pharisees and high priest or the people who sell medicine.

If we get any understanding from the example of the Apostle's lives and these words of Jesus, "pick up your cross and follow me," then we must understand that in a life that is a replica of Jesus there is going to be some crucifixions and stoning. This fact alone has probably caused many to recoil back from the call to live a life that is laid down for our neighbors. It is clear that this life caused these disciples to be stoned, crucified and beheaded for their actions of preaching a gospel that sounds like this. *"Love those who persecute you. Do good to those who do harm to you. Turn the other cheek. Give to anyone who asks of you. No greater love has anyone than that they lay down their life for their brother. You saw me hungry and you fed me. You saw me naked and you clothed me. Give and it shall be given to you. Forgive and you will be forgiven."*

We could go on all day with quotes like this. They define the nature of Jesus. He said that He came to reveal the Father. Should we then conclude that these words also revealed the nature of the Father?

If we want to represent the Father, we should be clothed in God's garments or armor, we should put on Jesus.

Chapter 6

WHAT DOES A JESUS REPLICA DO, EXACTLY?

STEPHEN, AFTER spending three years with Jesus was taken into the meeting of the council. He went for what reason, to accuse them? No, to preach the truth to them. *"Stephen, full of faith and power, did great wonders and signs among the people,"* then they argued with him. Here it is, the thing that got him killed, *"they were not able to resist the wisdom and the spirit by which he spoke."*

God in us, understanding this is a dangerous thing in the hands of a disciple who does not fear him who can only destroy our body. A disciple who instead values and honors Him who blesses our eternal soul, one who gives honor even to the point of hallowing His Name.

I do not get the impression that when these men were called and the only thing that they were told to do was "follow Me," they understood any part of the "pick up your cross" or the "lay down your life" conditions. However, it is obvious from just the story of Stephen that he figured it out.

Stephen had just seen Jesus crucified by these same men that he was addressing. He had only recently heard Jesus say "Father forgive them." Jesus had called His disciples "brothers" and "His Father their Father." He pleaded with them as "we" when referring to God and used the term "our Father" as a sign that God was their Father. Stephen knew who he had become. He had become a "fisher of men," he had become a replica of Jesus. Complete with Jesus' abilities to speak with wisdom and power.

Then Stephen told the council the truth and said that they had killed God's Holy Prophet again. This incited them and they went crazy and stoned him.

Before he died Stephen said, *"Lord do not charge them with this sin,"* just like Jesus did. If we are looking for a replica example, I cannot imagine a better one than Stephen. I can imagine the council of the Sanhedrin saying "did we not just kill this Jesus and here he is again in our face? Though he does appear in the bodily form of Stephen."

No one will pay for crucifying Jesus. No one will pay for stoning Stephen. Yes, Stephen does look a lot like Jesus. I can only imagine their first meeting in Heaven. Stephen might say "Lord it is my greatest pleasure to have died because of your name and to live forever by your side." Jesus might have replied, "It is my greatest pleasure to have watched as you lived, doing what I have taught you and representing me so well." "Enter in my good and faithful son."

Peter, James, John, Stephen and the others, these men who dropped all and left everything to follow Jesus are the greatest examples of what being Christian looks like. They believed that Jesus is the One, the Messiah. These men followed Him and spent their lives doing great feats of faith and risking all against tremendous odds. Giving their lives away to accomplish His purpose. Suffering the death of friends and finally giving their "last full measure of devotion," to quote Abraham Lincoln.

It is easy to define these disciples in terms like, 'not the sharpest knives in the drawer' and other descriptions that I have heard preachers use. Yet I believe these men are best described by their character and their resolve to live what they believe. These would be the attributes that would give the most accurate description of any man. How would any of us like to be defined by our every word or mistake? It seems Christians have a special knack for this as we call a man like Peter "impetuous" or Thomas "the doubter." If we would practice these principles of giving honor instead of taking honor we might call Stephen courageous, faithful, Stephen the merciful, Stephen the impersonator of Jesus.

Babe Ruth was called the "home run king" for many years of my life. Yet he struck out far more often than he hit home runs. Athletes get that kind of grace but disciples get labeled by their mistakes. Or their mis-spoken comments.

These men that left all to follow Jesus not only proved to be the "sharpest knives in the drawer" but they also proved to be the bravest of the brave and the most powerful men to have ever lived. They have affected the lives of some say, hundreds of millions of people, including me.

I read the words of Peter, John, James and Matthew and call their words the Word of God. I have followed them as they have followed Christ for nearly thirty four years, their example and their teachings have never led me astray.

Chapter 7

FOLLOW ME AS I FOLLOW CHRIST

I SAY these words to many people as a promise, if they would "follow me," I would follow Christ and lead them to safety. It seems like a strange thing to do. One of the groups that my wife and I and the staff and disciples of The Father's House Church in Oroville, California minister to is a group of people that are desperate to change the course of their lives but are helpless to do so. They have tried and have failed over and over. It is a most common statement to hear around The Father's House that a person believes that they have more failures in them but they feel they don't have any more recoveries in them. In other words the people at the church who are trying to escape an addictive and abusive lifestyle do not believe that they will survive any more trips through their past lives. We are hosting a memorial this week for one of our beloved brothers who proved to be correct on that feeling. Our work in the after care ministry to the addictive personalities is both fruitful and life threatening.

I am uneducated and I do not have experience in the world that they came from, jail, prison or addiction. Not to mention that I have been married thirty years and have been in love with one person who is the mother of all my children. Most of them have a completely different experience than I do.

Yet I make them this promise, "follow me and I will lead you out and you will like the future outcome of your life better than the past." I tell them "do what I do and say what I say, love who I love and trust who I trust." I am leading them in the imitation of Jesus. I tell them that my life is fashioned after my belief in what I think that Jesus is saying.

Jesus called me to "follow Him." I bowed my head and closed my eyes, I prayed a twenty second prayer and the next thing you know the world was a different place, God was real and it was Jesus who I had prayed to. I began to see that He wanted me to be like Him.

I gave my life to Jesus and then He hit me with the bombshell. He was not going to be my only teacher. He had disciples who were going to be placed in my life and He expected me to trust them, imitate them, even obey them, some of them proved to be imperfect, figure that. I pleaded with the Lord about this and He showed me that the men who wrote the Bible were imperfect and I follow them. The Lord even showed me that I called this book the Word of God. "Get back to the business of trusting in Me and the servants that I sent you," He told me. At first this was hard and I did not follow very well. I thought I was more perfect than my leaders were, which proved over and over that arrogance was a perfect breeding ground for independence. Independence, like the one member churches that spread all over the world and say things like all Christians are hypocrites and they have church when they go out to the wilderness. Most of them bear very little of the fruit of "laying ones life down for their brother" or "loving one another as I have loved you."

This is where I was headed when I remembered that all Jesus wanted from me was to "follow Him." Then I listened to His voice and read His word and found out that this independent spirit was not what He demonstrated. The men beating Him and crucifying Him were not His superiors, they were inferior in every way. He could have called Angels to destroy them and rescue Him but He submitted Himself even unto death. I remembered that nobody took His life from Him, He gave it willingly.

Just then His words came to my memory that "if anyone wishes to be great in His kingdom, they must be the servants of all. For the joy set before Him, He endured the cross," and this, "if there be any other way Father then let this cup pass from me, let thy will be done Father." Wow! Can I really imitate this Jesus? I'll try! I have tried, and I have given this challenge to the people who come to me to ask me to teach them how to escape from their bondage. Some people's bondage is to religion or their own way of thinking, mostly it is just very hard to submit to imperfect leaders and yield or surrender your will, yet, this is what Jesus is calling us to do.

My friend Ron is like this, caught in a cycle of drug use and selfishness that is very hard to escape. I remember the first day I that I saw him. He came to church because of a woman that he liked. He agreed to go to church with her but told her that if she stood up or lifted her hands or said anything, he was out of there. When he came to Jesus centered twelve step programs and anybody started talking about Jesus, Ron would say "this ain't church you know" and shame them or scare them into being quiet. Ron then went back to jail and had a relapse. He came out knowing just what I said earlier. He could not do this much longer. Ron knows that His life may be short, his body is breaking down.

I prayed with Ron to receive Jesus, it was a powerful introduction. Ron knew from that twenty seconds of prayer that God was real and that He had not rejected him.

My friend Ron is a bigger than life man who also stands about six foot four inches tall and is wide shouldered. He has a smile and a nature that is truly inviting and it has been said of Ron that he could sell ice to Eskimos.

Ron and I would have the follow me talks where we would identify the stumbling blocks in his life. I would tell him where, who and what would be dangerous for him. He would listen and agree. He really threw himself into this Christian living and soon became one of the brightest lights at The Father's House. He testified one day that his life was the best that it had ever been. You know, the next day Ron relapsed. You don't have to ask him if he has relapsed either, you can see it from down the road or hear it in his voice on the phone. He goes all in on his binges. His body will scream at him, it does not like methamphetamine at all, it hurts him. Eventually he came back and cried in repentance, begging God to forgive him and crying out for help and another chance. As we restore his life, all the addicts who ran to Ron during his relapse have to be removed from his house and all the paraphernalia destroyed.

Then we get on with healing the hurts of his heart. Dealing with the pain of his childhood. He had alcohol put in his baby bottle, he was called stupid and worthless, his brother was killed and Ron felt responsible. He was belittled and punished, even when he was good. He cries out in pain for help, not just physical pain either but soul pain like deep dark soul pain. We discuss what went wrong, asking how did this happen. I remind him, you said that your life was so good and you jumped back to the pain of hell. He tells how in secret he had begun to sneak away and do the things that I had told him not to do. Not big things, but little things like going to this place or that place, with this person or that person. Problem things with money which make him feel worthless, or getting himself involved with people who caused stress. People he may have even been trying to help but they were not ready. It may be something like trying to help someone who I had said he could not help because he was not ready to handle their failure or their accusations against him, which brings back the feelings of being less than that he felt as a child. He would decide that I was being unchristian and do the opposite of what I had told him. Also he would just talk himself into the thinking that I was wrong. When he wakes up in the life that he despised, or finds himself lost he comes back to find out is there another chance for him? Asking, has God rejected him? Have I rejected him? Well, we have not!

We discuss what happened and why. We talk through many mistakes and plan for his future success. Then we come to it, the question, "Ron are you ready to follow me?" He says "yes" and we begin. We have come to the testimony four times. He says, "this is the best my life has been." He then relapses, we try again.

Ron's story would convince anyone that God is in the business of loving the lost and giving hope to the hopeless. Ron was blind but now he sees, Ron was broken but now he is on the way to becoming whole, not again either, but for the first time. Yesterday I thought he was going to blow a gasket because of what I told him he had to do in his discipleship. Yet he yielded to the Lord and to me. Proclaimed again his trust in what God was doing in his life. I asked him right in the middle of the hardest day he had ever had in The Father's House to close his eyes and picture himself surrendering to the Lord, even raising his hand and saying the words "I surrender." Ron did this and I then said "when I lay hands on you the Holy Spirit will come upon you and He will baptize you with his power and a revelation of His love for you." I said "right now" as I laid my hand on his heart. I could feel what Ron was feeling, a surge of the Father's love for him. My friend began to cry as he fell into my arms, not tears of sadness but tears of joy and a relief that it was just like that first day way back when. Ron knew what I knew, that he was born again, again, and that God had not rejected him. He is my friend and my son in the way of our Father. I have said and will continue to say to him "follow me as I follow Christ and I promise you that I will lead you out."

I will continue to walk a very straight line because I have made this promise to do no harm and to deliver many into the hands of freedom and I will not use my freedoms as an excuse to forget the responsibility to love my brothers as I have been loved. I will lead them to freedom, which is to lead them to the love of God and His plan that He has set before them.

All I did was see that Jesus was real and heard His call to "follow

Me." Then I said "I will follow you and imitate you and be your disciple."

People would ask me all the time, "why do you keep taking Ron back?"I just answer them that if I want to be given second and third chances, then I have to give chances to the Ron's of the world and keep hoping and praying, loving them to the end. Repentance is the only condition. Ron is always repentant. So I will stay with the strugglers as long as they want to keep crying out to God. It took many years for them to reach the level of misery that they have reached. It will probably take a few to get them through all the circumstances that keep them enslaved.

There is a real chance that anyone who tries to minister to the addicted will lose heart and give up on these beautiful people, even losing faith because of their struggles and even failures, often taking these relapses as the failure of God or the failure of our faith. It is their choice, they have to choose and no matter how much I want to choose for them I cannot choose for them. Each one must answer the call of Jesus to "follow Me." Some will not.

To accept the call of Jesus to "follow Me," then to accept the responsibility to live a life that others can follow to get them out of whatever has them held in bondage is always dependent on the other person's free will. They get to choose. If you think that I am only talking about addicts then you would be mistaken. The life of faith and love is challenged by more things than addictions.

Chapter 8

APPLES GROWING ON ORANGE TREES

MANY MORE people are trusting in something other than God. They trust in things like life insurance and savings accounts not to mention paychecks and property equity. Anything that takes your trust and faith away from God or puts Him in a position in your life that is anything other than first, is sin and some even say idolatry. Repentance is the cure. It should be sorrowful repentance, because we should be sorry when we miss the mark, as sin is so often defined as.

This brings me to repentance being defined as the turning away from what is being repented for! Sin, which should be what we repent of, being defined as 'missing the mark.' I have been often asked, "how do you know that someone has repented?" I think that in the long run you have to know that only God and the person who is repenting will really know. I do have to have some standard to look for and the one I have chosen is the one I learned from "listening to

Him." I examine the fruit of it.

What does the fruit look like you may ask! I might answer that question by telling you that the fruit of repentance would be turning away from the thing that held them enslaved. This thing is usually selfish based and always resists submission. This fruit would at least look as though they have turned away from it. I ask the questions, are they doing what it takes to be far from their past life? And, are they aiming at what is right? It always seems like false repentance if they are not taking careful aim at what is right. The only way to have a chance at hitting the target is to aim at the target. I look to see, is there evidence of the fruit that they are aiming?

Seeing if a person is aiming at the right outcome is the fruit to me and I would give that person as many chances as I want God to give to me. If a person is not trying to hit the mark there would be fruit for that as well. They might be living a double life or making excuses. The fruit is always what it should be. I own an orange grove and it is as you might imagine full of orange trees. If the trees were not full of oranges it would be evidence that something is wrong here. It could be that my information is wrong, I only thought that it was an orange tree. If I look at this orange tree and apples are growing then either this was not an orange tree or someone has done some horticultural finagling on it and it stopped being a orange tree. The fact is that "you know the tree by its fruit." You get what you are supposed to get. With people, it is different, what you see is not always what you get. You must learn to look at the fruit.

In the story of the sheep and goats in Matthew chapter 25 Jesus tells that the Kingdom will be gathered and separated by the fact of whether they are sheep or goats. Jesus will say that these are sheep because they did something for Jesus. They fed Him or visited Him, gave Him something to drink or took Him in off of the street. Each group, the ones who did and the ones who did not, questioned the Lord with the words when did we or when did we not?. He answered them that it was when they did it or did not do it to one of the least of these His brothers. The fruit that Jesus was looking for was the fruit of who did it to the least of these His brothers. The results were that He separated the farm animals based on the fruit that they had produced.

Jesus is going to say that you are a sheep and you go over there, you are a goat so go over there. He put them in two groups. Then the story goes on to say that Jesus is going to send the goats to "eternal punishment" and the sheep to "eternal life." Now lets recap, "eternal life" or "eternal punishment" based on the fruit we bore in life. The fruit bearers question the fruit, as if they did not know that this was the fruit that He was going to look for. If I knew what you were looking for I would have grown the right fruit. Apples don't grow on orange trees and goats don't look like sheep. When I stand before God when the Kingdom is gathered together and it is time to separate the sheep from the goats, I will tell you one thing for sure, I do not want to be mistaken for a goat. I want to sound like a sheep and look like a sheep, I want my hair to be sheep like and my hooves and my wool to be sheep like. No mistake, if you inspect me I will be sheep. If Jesus was using orange trees I would want to be the perfect orange, perfect color and size with the sweetest juice possible. No yellowing of the skin or bitterness so that I could be mistaken as a lemon. If the King of Heaven and Lord over all of the Earth, who is my Father in Heaven, is going to judge the fruit of my life based on whether I did or did not do something then I want to be doing that something and not look like someone who does not do it.

I have found that in following Jesus there are invaluable methods for avoiding the time wasters and the fakers who are sent to rob, kill and destroy. Not to mention the people who want something like a magic fix of their problems and are just not ready and may never be ready to escape the madness and embrace the love of the Father. I have never been perfect but my results in helping them to truth and love have greatly increased by inspecting the fruit of their lives. If they fool me or I just grow weary in my efforts to do good by them, then the end result will be misery, at least until they come around again for another try (if they can that is).

Our struggle for the lives of the sheep, our producing baby sheep, our ensuring that they will be found to be sheep, is a life of tries and failure, starts and stops. It is made fruitful and abundantly so by the revelation that apples don't grow on orange trees, that sheep don't look like goats and the separation of them is seen easily by what they do.

If you are following someone then you should inspect the fruit of their life and you will find that the fruit will tell you if you can trust their judgement. The fruit should be the characteristics of Jesus like mercy and kindness. The fruit of the spirit should be evident as well.

If you are leading people you should consider making a commitment to live a life that someone could imitate. Keeping your household in order and your business dealings honest. If someone were to look into your secret life would you be the same person in secret as you are in public?

You should be confident as you tell them that you will imitate Jesus, so they are safe to imitate you. You should know that if they look closely at you they will see the fruit that you are supposed to be.

In my life I want to be inspected by those who are trusting me to lead them out. At The Father's House we have many relapses and miserably failed attempts at getting the Father's purpose for life instilled in someone's life. They fail at being loved. "*For God so loved the world, that He gave His only begotten Son, that whosoever believes in Him shall not perish, but have eternal life.*" God's love was the purpose of Jesus and God's love is the purpose for our lives. I want people to know that they can come back to me and find the real deal here at The Father's House. If they fall back, then they know where to come back to, to get started again. We invite fruit inspection and we guard against insincere examples of leadership.

The right fruit on the right tree, sincerity and honor, patience and goodness, these are the fruit of the seeker of God's grace and peace. Repentance and an effort to hit the mark must be in the tree if the fruit is going to be what you want it to be.

Apples on Apple trees and Oranges on Orange trees just like they are supposed to be. The Apostles had to look like Jesus replicas or we should not have followed their lead. Jesus said that they would do the things that He did and greater things than these would they do, and they did too. They were the fruit of His life here on earth and good fruit they were too. All Christian leaders and all Christian followers should learn from the fact that Jesus took twelve men and taught them by example for three years, leading them and telling them the truth. Jesus showed them servanthood by washing their feet and said that it was the road to greatness. He showed the power by praying for people and He told them to do it also. He showed them sacrifice by submitting Himself even unto death on a cross. Jesus made it clear to them that they would suffer for His name's sake and history tells that they did too. We today must answer the call of Jesus to "follow Him" and submit ourselves to the call to imitate Him, telling His story using words as well as actions to offer ourselves as a "living sacrifice unto Him."

You will always find Apples on Apple trees and Oranges on Orange trees and you will always find servanthood, goodness and a serious effort to do right and good, on every tree that does more than say that they are Christians. They will trust God in their finances and be generous givers. I am not talking about perfect people but sincere people who are aiming at the target and trying to hit the mark.

These are some of the principles of following and leading that are often overlooked or forgotten. Not finding them in one's life could be one reason that people don't want to see Christianity as "the way, truth and life" solution that it is claimed to be by its practitioners. We say what the fruit is on every venue available, then we as Christian leaders want to excuse ourselves from being tested for the presence of the fruit of what we claimed was there.

The follower hears that the fruit is there but does not examine the fruit and wonders why they do not see the promised results.

The fruit that is supposed to be there has to be understood and clearly stated in every venue available. It is the fruit of the Holy Spirit, the promise of the Father fulfilled. "*And behold, I am sending forth the promise of My Father upon you; but you are to stay in the city until you are clothed with power from on high.*" The Holy Spirit and power are the promise of the Father, this is the fruit of the Christian life. "*But the fruit of the Spirit is love, joy, peace, patience, kindness, goodness, faithfulness, gentleness, self-control; against such things there is no law.*" These are the fruit of the promise of the Father. I should be examining my life and the life of those I listen to or follow to see that the fruit of the Spirit is evident. These fruit being the target, the aiming at the target being the evidence that is important. Are we and our leaders aiming at the targets that are important? Is the fruit of the Spirit growing on the Spirit filled trees of our lives?

Apples grow on Apple trees and faith, love and hope grow on people who are aiming to grow them. It is evident in how we deal with our money and how we deal with our relationships. It is evident in what we value. It is evident as we answer the question, do we live our lives for us or do we live our lives for others? Spiritual fruit on spiritual men, just like Apples and Oranges.

Chapter 9

YOU CANNOT BE MY DISCIPLE

"Now LARGE *crowds were going along with Him; and He turned and said to them,"*

"*If anyone comes to Me, and does not hate his own father and mother and wife and children and brothers and sisters, yes, and even his own life, he cannot be My disciple.*"

"*Whoever does not carry his own cross and come after Me cannot be My disciple.*"

"*For which one of you, when he wants to build a tower, does not first sit down and calculate the cost to see if he has enough to complete it?*"

"*Otherwise, when he has laid a foundation and is not able to finish, all who observe it begin to ridicule him, saying, 'This man began to build and was not able to finish'.*"

"*Or what king, when he sets out to meet another king in battle, will not first sit down and consider whether he is strong enough with ten thousand men to encounter the one coming against him with twenty thousand?"*

"Or else, while the other is still far away, he sends a delegation and asks for terms of peace."

"So then, none of you can be My disciple who does not give up all his own possessions."

"Therefore, salt is good; but if even salt has become tasteless, with what will it be seasoned?"

"It is useless either for the soil or for the manure pile; it is thrown out. He who has ears to hear, let him hear."

Jesus says that it is possible to not qualify as His disciple when He says, "you cannot be My disciple." He gives many examples, but I was quite amazed after thirty years of preaching and teaching to have such a revelation as this.

It is possible to not qualify to be His disciple. Jesus says it as plain as day, "you cannot be My disciple."

Like, if you love your wife or children more than Him.

Or if you love your father and mother more than Him.

If you don't give up all your possessions.

If you don't pick up your cross and follow Him. This could mean not imitate or not do what He says. Like not obey maybe.

Then He says that we should count the cost before we accept the title of disciple. He uses building a tower as the first example then goes on to liken it to a king trying to decide to go to war. If you can't win don't fight. If you can't finish don't start.

The "you cannot be My disciple" words are just ringing in my ears. He is talking to the people who were traveling with Him. He said it to people who wanted to be His disciple. I want to be His disciple, don't you? It reminds me of the question He previously asked, *"why do you call Me Lord and do not do what I have commanded."* Here He says that people who are not what He describes, "cannot be My disciple." It is scary to think that humans can be disqualified from salvation be-cause they love their children, wives, mothers and fathers too much, or because they just cannot pick up the cross and all that it means.

What about all the other litmus tests that we have put on the evaluation of whether or not a person is a Christian?

When I was first saved back in the 1970's long hair was a sign of rebellion. One lady that I knew was told to choose between roller skating and Jesus. The standard of music was that if it had much beat it was of the devil.

What I am getting from this is that no matter how far we are willing to move the line, there is a line and on one side of the line there is the chance of it being said of us by Jesus that "you cannot be My disciple."

In today's church it seems that we want to make everything okay just because we want it to be so, and we want our freedom too. In some circles it does not matter what a man does, it is more important how much anointing he has. I have seen people call the ability to hype "anointing," so that would mean that the line is set based on hype, or on a trained ability to rhyme words together, or a willingness to proclaim something a miracle without any evidence at all. Which in my opinion makes a miracle a very unmiraculous thing. The reason for doing this is to give the impression of anointing so as to be able to exercise freedom and not have anyone question it. The absolutely astonishing part is that there is a line that must not be crossed, the penalty for crossing it is that Jesus says, "you cannot be My disciple."

Where is the line? This is the question that should be asked. Is it really a line that we can see or actually know? How far is too far in pre-marital sex and how much alcohol is too much? How much skin should a woman show in public, what jokes are too dirty and how crude can a joke be? Secular music? What about R rated movies? So many questions, where are the answers? What is the line that determines can and cannot be Jesus' disciple? Roller skating, poker playing, tattoos and piercing have all been used in my somewhat brief life as descriptions of the line and there are so many more.

The line is somewhere and Jesus made it very clear in these verses. Most people that I talk to say that they are safely on the right side of the line because they "believe." These people are not told that the test is in their belief, Jesus just says that unless you can answer these questions right then "you cannot be My disciple."

Where is that line?

The answer from me is that I don't have the answer for you.

The Father does, and he told Peter, James and John on a mountain that we call transfiguration to "listen to Him" and everyone knew that He meant Jesus.

Jesus also said that the line was that you must *"forgive or you will not be forgiven."* He also said that if you see the "least of these" hungry and you do not feed them that you would be a goat. It does not turn out so good for goats.

Jesus also mentions naked, thirsty, strangers and imprisoned people in the sheep and goats story of Matthew 25.

If we would study the teachings of Jesus as the instructions of the Father and "listen to him," we would probably be so busy with the hungry, naked, thirsty people, all the while preaching the kingdom to the "ends of the earth" and "in every nation," (including our own) that we would just find ourselves over on the right side anyways.

Jesus said *"A new commandment I give to you, that you love one another, even as I have loved you, that you also love one another. "By this all men will know that you are My disciples, if you have love for one another."*

People looking on would say "those must be Jesus' disciples, see how they love their neighbors and one another." I do have the answer for me, it is listen to Jesus. Whatever that looks like I should be spending more than a ho-hum amount of effort on finding what that standard requires.

Here in this verse that says "you cannot be My disciple" Jesus says that it was loving him more than our children and our wives.

I remember back in 1979 when I was getting married and I already knew that Jesus said that I must love Him the most. My bride to be, Vicki said to me,"it is so great that we will always be each others number one." To which I replied "I am sorry Vicki but you can never be my number one." I saw the stinging look of surprise on her face, so I continued and explained, "the Lord has to be my number one so that you do not become an idol to me and that would put our life and marriage in jeopardy." I went on to tell her that if God called us to some other part of the world, we would go. Even if there was danger and hardship. We must be willing to "follow Him."

The churchy answer was that God would not do that. The biblical answer is that He did send Jesus to the cross, Steven to the Sanhedrin and Paul to the Romans. He would send me to Oroville and expect me to lay down my life for my neighbor.

I remember in those days (the 1970's) there were many discussions about the imminent return of the Lord, questioning whether you were ready or not. The question is answered by a question, are you a disciple of Jesus? Do you love Him more than yourself or your mother, father, wife or children? Are you willing to pick up the cross and die for your neighbor? Remember, that the standard of imitating Jesus is that He died not just for those who were good to Him, but for those who were driving the nails in His hands, spitting in His face and falsely accusing Him. Jesus must be on the throne of my life. I must love Him more than all, so that I can qualify to be a disciple of Jesus,and keep everything and everyone in my life under the covering of the Father. Anyone I love more is above Him and not under the covering. Not protected. No wonder marriages and families of Christian people suffer so much brokenness, they are targets of the enemy.

I must also be willing to "pick up the cross" and follow or imitate Him, learning from His example and doing what I see Him do and what I hear Him say.

If you don't count the cost, don't start the project. If you don't have the ability to win don't start the fight. Being a disciple of Jesus takes great effort, even planning and forethought.

It also takes a power that makes the battle winnable. If you can't finish don't start and if you cannot win don't fight (surrender is the point). This being a disciple is a project.

So the question is "WHERE IS THE LINE" that determines if you can or cannot be Jesus' disciple?

My opinion is that finding the line should be one of our most deliberate and constant efforts, always soul searching, always hearing the voice of God as He says, "this is the way" or "that is the way." When we find the line, then we should give it as much room as we can. Not seeing how close we can get to the line but instead seeing how far we can get from the line. The question often asked of me, how far is too far with my girlfriend? We should not be asking how close to the line we are allowed to get. Instead we should be setting a standard that is away from the line. In fact I should be making a Steve shaped hole in the wall in an effort to get away from that line and set a new standard for myself.

If I determine that something is not a disqualifying action, my next question should be, does it cause my brother to stumble?

Jesus says in Matthew, Mark and Luke that if we cause our brother to stumble it would be better if a huge millstone were hung around our neck and we were drowned in the sea.

Most of the reasons that people have for their behavior and where they have drawn the line is that they have the freedom. They say, "I am not under law" or "all things are lawful to me."

What we forget in this equation is the caused stumbling of our brother. We forget the millstone around the neck, and the casting into the sea that follows. These verses should not be forgotten when we are discussing this freedom as a tool for positioning the line. The words that are used by Jesus to describe the stumbling block that we are supposed to avoid becoming are the same words that are used to describe the bait that one uses to lure the prey into the trap.

Where the line is that says you can or you cannot be His disciple should be considered often, since it was Jesus that brought up the subject.

Chapter 10

ARE YOU SALTY?

THE NEXT words in Luke's gospel are these, *"therefore, if salt has lost its saltiness."* The word "Therefore" connects the two subjects.

How does this relate in a talk about what disqualifies one from being a disciple?

Jesus tells us to love Him the most, to pick up our cross and be willing to die for our brother, to sell all of our possessions. He says that if a builder does not count the cost or a king does not decide if he is strong enough to win before he fights, "therefore" (or because of these facts,) "if salt has lost its saltiness" it is "useless."

What could this mean? What does salt have to do with these previous points? Obviously they do since Jesus said "therefore" just before he said "if salt has lost its saltiness." You could substitute the words "If disciples quit being disciply."

What is the saltiness that we could lose it? Salt today is used for flavor more than anything, in Jesus' day it was as well. It was also a preservative, it would keep meat from spoiling. When you get teeth pulled you wash your mouth with salt and it promotes healing, it cleanses the sore. So, if we just stop there with the obvious we have healing, cleansing, preserving and flavoring.

Would it be right to then conclude that since Jesus included salt in his description of the standard that would determine if you qualify as a disciple, that these attributes of salt are what is expected of a disciple? Would it mean that if a disciple is present then there would be healing and flavor? That right things like love, acceptance and forgiveness would be preserved? Maybe the flavor of Jesus would be tasted by those who live around disciples. Salt shakers would be around for people to use to flavor their lives. When people see how much disciples like the taste of their lives, people would say "pass the salt please." That is all good except when they don't like what they see in the disciple's lives, then they say "no thank you" to Jesus.

In our churches do we have healing, cleansing, preserving, seasoning? Do we, promote the spreading of the gospel? Thereby preserving the message of the gospel? Just by our presence alone do we make things better?

If salt has lost its flavor or seasoning "it is useless." Useless really?

Lets recap, "You cannot be My disciple."

If you don't love him the most, (including everyone).

If you cannot pick up the cross and follow (obey, right?).

If you cannot finish what you started.

If you try but cannot win the battle.

The big one, if you cannot give up all your possessions.

If you are salt that does not be salty (heal, flavor, preserve or cleanse), Jesus says that you would be "useless." It has been my conclusion that we should listen to Jesus. He really is the one who has the final say in this.

Here He says these most incredible things about the qualifications of being His disciple. None of which mention believing or saying that you are a disciple.

The answer to the question. "How do I know that I am on the right side of the line," is this, follow the teachings of Jesus, doing what He says and believing His promises. Ask yourself first the question, do I look like Jesus' description of a disciple? Or do I disqualify myself, would Jesus say to me "You cannot be My disciple?"

I think that a review of Jesus' prayers in the Gospel of John would be a good thing to do while you search for this answer, asking yourself the following questions.

Am I baptized in repentance, have I turned around? Is "go and sin no more" my standard? It is the only standard acceptable to a disciple of Jesus who answers the call of Jesus to "follow Me."

Do I have revelation of the Father? He came to show me the Father, did I get what Jesus was showing me? Jesus came to show forth His Father's name to us, do I Have His name revealed to me? Jesus said that He and His Father would make their home in us, is He the Present One in me?

Have I understood or at least accepted the incredible suffering that comes with the cross? This is the price that Jesus paid. Sin has a price and I did not have to pay it, He was broken, so that I don't have to be. Am I willing to "pick up the cross and follow Him?"

Since Jesus used the term "therefore" and connected these two subjects, "you cannot be My disciple" and "if salt has lost its saltiness," I think it would be wise to look at our lives and answer the question, "am I salty?"

Chapter 11

YOU ARE MY FRIENDS IF YOU DO WHAT I COMMAND YOU

IT IS clear that the teacher and master of who can be Jesus' disciple is Jesus Himself. He declares it when He says, *"By this all men will know that you are My disciples," "that you love one another." "No greater love has any man than that he lay down his life for his brother."*

He makes it clear that there is fruit that will be visible to others that will make this obvious. This fruit is that we would "love one another." Now as if that is not enough he has to add "as I have loved you." The outcome would be that "they would know that you are My disciples."

Since Jesus says that there is a standard by which you "cannot be My disciple," it is very important to remember that there is a standard by which it is possible to easily see if you are his disciple.

How does a person love their brother as Jesus has loved us? Jesus tells us a parable. When one guy asked Jesus "who is my neighbor?" Jesus answered with the story of the good Samaritan. In this story he tells of a man who is Jewish being beaten by robbers and left in a ditch. Along came Jewish people and they pass by because they have their own problems. Then a man comes along, who is considered as less than a dog by the man in the ditch. The man who helped was a Samaritan. Now as he helped the man in the ditch, he gave his time, his money and care, showing love and even promising future care and money, regardless of this Jewish man's opinion of him.

Then Jesus asked his questioner, "*who was a neighbor to this man?*" "*The one who had mercy on him*" was the answer. Jesus then said "*go and do likewise.*" All of this as an answer to the question "how do I get eternal life?"

Jesus was constantly telling stories and giving examples of loving people more than you love law and self. Looking out for the pain and bondage of others. Being a preserving, healing, cleansing, flavoring presence in the world and all of these defined as love.

Seven times he healed on the sabbath asking the question "*is it good to heal this man on the sabbath?*" Jesus said about one woman that He healed on the sabbath that these scribes and Pharisees would let their ox out and set it free to eat on the sabbath but they don't think that the Father would want to set a person that He loves free on the sabbath.

Jesus says that there is a standard set that will determine that, "you cannot be My disciple." He also says that it will be obvious to all men that "you are My disciple," if you "love one another as I have loved you." We should "listen to Him" and only "listen to Him."

The words of Jesus will determine if we are his disciples. He says that His words will judge us in John chapter 12. I will listen and make it my life's pursuit to be His disciple and obey His call to "follow Me."

Chapter 12

WHAT IS THIS MURDER ABOUT?

"FOR THE joy set before Him He endured the cross" and "*no greater love has anyone than that he lay down his life for his brother.*"

Jesus laid down His life for me, paying a debt that I could not pay, a debt that He did not owe. He endured the cross, and a beating so severe that He did not resemble a man. It is good to reflect on the suffering of Jesus from time to time so as not to forget what "loving one another" meant to Him.

I grew up in a church that had Jesus on the cross. There He was, all the time, right there in front of me. I asked God, who I thought was a very distant God, "what is this murder about?" I would also ask "why," because I was very confused.

Nails, spears, thorns and a severe beating, it is clear that He knew what was coming. In fact, the night before this crucifixion, He prayed that if He could accomplish His mission in some other way then let it be so. "Your will, not mine" was a clear statement that He accepted the plan. To save us, He had to endure the cross. We were the joy set before Him, our salvation and our return to a relationship with the Father was His joy.

If that was not enough He then gave us the status of "joint heirs," in other words we get what He earned. Then the promise of "doing the works that He did" and "even greater things than these will you do."

Plus this, "*as many as received Him, to them He gave the right to become children of God, even to those who believe in His name.*"

Is there no end to His love for us? He not only tells us how to have eternal life, then He shares his position in eternity with us. All for the price of loving our neighbor as He has loved us. He then shows us at the cross, in a very real way how to lay down your life for each other and He says that if we do this, this will be the evidence that we are His disciples.

All Jesus asks of us is that we should love one another as He has loved us. When translated in English this means that I would give my life away for the blessing of others and that I would forgive others as Jesus has forgiven me.

Everything that I do in relation to finding out where the line is, to find out if I qualify as I "can" or I "cannot be His disciple" will be determined by how I deal with these two imitations of Jesus. Do I love as He loved, laying down my life? Do I forgive as I want to be forgiven? I will continue to look at these two questions, examining the words of Jesus to see if He has any more litmus tests that reveal the answer for me.

What this murder is about is explained by the great plan which was in place for the purpose of restoring our relationship to God as our Father. A relationship that Adam and Eve had in the garden. Since man has sinned he is separated from God and Jesus came as "the Lamb of God" to "take away the sins of the world." The brutality of this murder was to cleanse any man who has accepted the suffering and sacrifice of Jesus in their place. Allowing His suffering to take the place of us suffering for our sins.

The motive for this is stated so clearly in this verse *"for God so loved the world he gave His only Son."* It is God's love that sent Jesus to the cross and this is what this murder is about.

What determines if this love is enough to save me is found in my response to Jesus' words, His words about loving, laying down my life and the conditions of being His disciple.

Chapter 13

WITH CHRIST IN THE SCHOOL OF DISCIPLESHIP

SINCE IT is clear that Jesus came and endured the cross for the purpose of saving us and restoring us to the love of the Father, I think we should take seriously the commands of Jesus which He said would reveal that we are His disciples.

What did Jesus want those of us who have answered His call to "Follow Me" to do ? Let's look for the answer in some of Jesus' own words.

"*But when the Pharisees heard that Jesus had silenced the Sadducees, they gathered themselves together. One of them, a lawyer, asked Him a question, testing Him, Teacher, which is the great commandment in the Law? And He said to him, YOU SHALL LOVE THE LORD YOUR GOD WITH ALL YOUR HEART, AND*

WITH ALL YOUR SOUL, AND WITH ALL YOUR MIND. This is the great and foremost commandment. The second is like it, YOU SHALL LOVE YOUR NEIGHBOR AS YOURSELF. On these two commandments depend the whole Law and the Prophets."

And again,

"Little children, I am with you a little while longer You will seek Me; and as I said to the Jews, now I also say to you, Where I am going, you cannot come. A new commandment I give to you, that you love one another, even as I have loved you, that you also love one another. By this all men will know that you are My disciples, if you have love for one another."

"Simon Peter said to Him, Lord, where are You going? Jesus answered, Where I go, you cannot follow Me now; but you will follow later. Peter said to Him, Lord, why can I not follow You right now? I will lay down my life for You."

"Jesus answered, "Will you lay down your life for Me? Truly, truly, I say to you, a rooster will not crow until you deny Me three times."

I have asked twelve adult Christians this week, what did Jesus command of us? I expected the answer that I got. All twelve said "love the Lord your God with all your heart, mind, soul and strength. Love your neighbor as you love yourself." All twelve said this and probably most Christians believe that this is correct. Yet when you look up Jesus' answer that people are quoting, you find out that Jesus is answering the question of how a Jewish man fulfills the law.

When you look up the commands that Jesus gave to His disciples you find the words, *"this I command you, that you love one another as I have loved you."* Also you find that Jesus says *"by this all men will know that you are My disciples."* Just one command and then as you look further, you find one condition, that you *"believe in the one that the Father sent."* Love as He loved and believe. Faith and love, they go together over and over in the teachings of the disciples, as they commend the believers for their faith and love.

This love my neighbor as I love myself is hard enough. Jesus told the rich young ruler that he had to sell all that he had and give it to the poor, or you could translate it to mean his neighbors. I have asked many times, why this guy was told this and not every one that Jesus met? Jesus said this in answer to the statement by the rich young ruler that he had obeyed the ten commandment all of his life. Jesus said "you still lack one thing," as in one thing to be able to say that you had obeyed the commandments all of your life. I think He is saying you have bought many things and comforts for yourself, now go and buy them for your neighbor and then you can say that you loved your neighbor as yourself. Yet even then you still lack what you need for eternal life. Jesus then told him the really hard thing for all rich young rulers to do. Jesus said "come and follow Me," just as He had told the disciples. The very same call to the rich man as the poor man.

When I was young I would ask how could I possibly go to Heaven? The answer turned out to be "come and follow me." This come and follow me answer to the question, how do I get eternal life, is the very simple instruction that Jesus gave this man. I believe, as we have seen, that He gave this instruction throughout the Gospels. This is a subject that we need to study when we "listen to Him" as the Father told us on the Mount of Transfiguration.

What Jesus is saying here when He says that He gives us a new command is different. It says that we should love one another as we have been loved. This is a totally different premise. To love as I love myself is not always pretty and causes me to require justice and repayment in my life for wrongs that I have suffered. To love as I have been loved is to "forgive as I have been forgiven." To provide as I have been provided for, and to "give as it has been given to me," freely, without the requirements of repayment. This is a different standard. I said earlier that there is only one command and one condition. There really is only one. When I love as I have been loved I do fulfill all of the law as well as the command of Christ.

The words that Jesus said, "*I have come to fulfill the law not to abolish it,*" make a whole lot more sense now. To love as I have been loved and forgive as I have been forgiven, heal as I have been healed, serve as I have been served, really does make me an imitator of Jesus.

It would qualify me as coming in His name and the things that I do would be greater than the things that He did. Imitating Him would make me like Him, since He loved as He was loved and only did what the Father showed Him to do, He only said what the Father told Him to say. His will was to do the will of His Father.

If I am to love as I have been loved, I would love as the Father loved me, since He *"so loved the world that He gave His only son."* He so loved me that He gave His Son? So, do I give my son? Jesus so loved me that He endured the cross. He loved His purpose and His obedience to the Father more than His mother, brothers and sisters. Jesus did pick up His cross and "for the joy set before Him" He did "endure the cross." Should I then pick up my cross? Is that the answer to the eternal life question? Jesus said that it was and these subjects are related. They are related as soon as you add the words of Jesus, *"the one who obeys me, He is the one who loves me."* Is it "loves me as I have loved them?" Is that the "obeys me" that Jesus is referring to? That we would obey His "new command," to love as we have been loved?

Crosses, stoning and insults, whips, beatings and hardships. Are these the deals that our beloved brothers, the disciples of Christ accepted when they answered the call to "come and follow Me?" Is this what I agree to when I say that I will follow Him? Or is prosperity and comfort the end result of a life given over to following? Just ask yourself, what did Jesus have? The answer is that *"foxes have holes and birds of the air have nests but the Son of Man has nowhere to lay His head."* What does this command, *"love one another as I have loved you"* mean? It means follow Jesus and when you feel that you have understood how you have been loved so lavishly, then go and do likewise to your neighbor.

In any discussion about imitating Jesus, the subject of forgiveness must be included. Jesus majored on the subject of forgiveness. When he taught us how to pray in Matthew chapter 6, He said that we should include in our prayer the request that we be forgiven of our sins. Then He threw the monkey wrench in the whole deal with the request that we be forgiven only as we forgive those who have sinned against us. After the instructions on prayer Jesus continues on the subject of forgiveness saying "*For if you forgive others for their transgressions, your heavenly Father will also forgive you, but if you do not forgive others, then your Father will not forgive your transgressions.*"

I really wish He had not said that. It really complicates things for me. In the 18th chapter of Matthew, Jesus tells of a guy who did not forgive as he had been forgiven. When the forgiving master hears of it He puts the forgiven sins back on this man. Then Jesus goes on to says this, "*My heavenly Father will also do the same to you, if each of you does not forgive his brother from your heart.*" Jesus' Father will put the sins back on me if I don't "forgive as I have been forgiven." I will pay for every one of them. It does not sound like an option, I wonder why I have not heard this preached very often, if the sins of my past can be put back on me if I forget to "forgive as I have been forgiven?" I have in recent years heard a great deal about this from John and Carol Arnott since they have been preaching this all over the world. I am very grateful to them for bringing this message to me and I would recommend their book, *The Importance of Forgiveness*, as the best book on this subject that I know of. I wrote extensively about it in a book that I wrote called *Living and Loving Jesus* where I included a transcript of a sermon on this subject. I have often said that this is the most ignored subject in the church today and I have since found another one. It is the subject of the command of Christ to "love one another as I have loved you." The best book on this subject that I have read is called *Love Revolution*, by Gaylord Enns. These books need to be read by everyone who would be "With Christ in the School of Discipleship." They are truly the most ignored subjects in Christianity today and the most important. Jesus said "*why do you call Me Lord and do not do what I have commanded.*" Plus "*My heavenly Father will also do the same to you, if each of you does not forgive his brother from your heart.*" What could be more important to anyone who would answer the call of Jesus to "follow Me."

Chapter 14

VICKI THEN

VICKI LASORELLA was raised in a religion that had made her feel distant from God. This church gave one no sense that God was real. Yet it would leave you with a feeling of wanting to know. Is this real? Is He real? Do I even matter to Him? Is He mad at me? What young people like Vicki do is try not to think about it. They think I am young and when I get old maybe then I will need what this religion can give me.

She went about her life looking for what would make her feel good. The usual things like boy friends and social relationships. Trying to be cool and accepted into the world around her.

When I met Vicki we were 15 and 16 years old. She was my cousin's cousin and she was Mrs. Personality. She lit up every room that she was in, hardly anyone did not notice Vicki. I can tell you right where I was standing when I first laid eyes on her. We became friends exactly seconds after we met.

It was 1972 and my sister was getting married. My aunt and uncle came to the wedding with their six kids and their niece from Chicago.

All of the cousins played and ran around together using this wedding week as a chance to spend quality time together. Since my parents home would only accommodate the adults, all of the kids slept out in the yard, which was a lot of fun. We played the game Marco Polo in the pool which is a game where the one who is 'it' shuts their eyes and swims around saying Marco and everyone else says Polo. The 'it' person tries to touch someone and guess who it was that they touched. I would try to be 'it' and would always cheat. I would peak so that I could find Vicki and touch her.

Vicki and I wrote each other for years and since there were no cell phones, fax machines and certainly no computers or Facebook we had to use the U.S. Mail. It was slow and eventually we lost touch but I never forgot her. When we got older, one of those cousins got married. Since they were my cousin and hers, Vicki and I ended up at the same place again. This time we were 18 and 19 years old. This time we got romantic and began a relationship. I went home from this wedding definitely in love with Vicki LaSorella.

She was so impressed with me that soon after this, she began a relationship with a guy in Spokane that lasted four years.

I on the other hand never got her out of my mind. We wrote back and forth for a while and then I had the experience that changed both of our lives forever.

Chapter 15

THE WORLD WAS A DIFFERENT PLACE

ON MARCH 10th, 1975 I went to a free concert where a rock band named Sweet Comfort was playing. Their motive was to play their music and preach Jesus to people.

It is funny how the Lord calls people to follow Him. I was not looking for Him. I was very angry about religion and God or any subject concerning His love for me.

When my brother came home trying to tell me about Jesus loving me and that God had a plan for me, I was just plain disgusted. Really, I wanted to hate him but I did not know how. If he was around my parents house for even a day I would want to beat him. If he was gone back to college I would miss him. You see he had always been the life of the party. My brother was the first to get me drunk, the first to give me pot to smoke. It was hanging out with him at colleges that caused me to be sexually active. He was the coolest of the cool, he even had great nicknames and very close friends, I was so impressed.

When he would come home preaching that Jesus is real and that God has made a way for me to know Him I thought that he was an idiot.

It was not the first time that I had heard about Jesus. I had secretly watched Katherine Kulman for years. I had Christian young people try to tell me on many occasions that God loved me. I hatefully responded on every occasion.

You see, I had grown up in the same church that Vicki had grown up in. I had never met anyone who had lived their faith, at least not in a way that I could tell. I had thought that the priests were married to God so they must be true, then one day I was mistakenly let into the priest's house and there was pornography and alcohol everywhere. As a young impressionable boy I was so disillusioned that I was not going to believe in these Christians again!

There I was at this Christian concert in Stockton, California. The musicians talked about the fact that God wants to know you, they said that He cares about you and that you could know Him. At this point every person who had not lived their faith faded from the landscape of my thoughts. I went forward like a zombie. I don't know how I got to the front, I only know that in an auditorium of many people, I was the only one to come forward.

I came to my senses and started to back track as the young man from the band was trying to tell me how to meet the Lord. I told him that it was no use. I was not 'monk' material. His name was Bryan and he simply asked me "if God were real would you follow Him, would you let Him change you?" Bryan went on to tell me that if I would pray with him, God would let me know that He was real. I said "if He is real I want to know."

You see, that is all that I had ever wanted to know. The church that I was raised in was so boring that I had plenty of time to talk to God, to read the Gospel stories that were in the monthly handouts. Each year they would take us around to these raised sculptures of the different situations of Calvary and they called these the Stations of the

Cross. While you are young and sitting through church so bored that you wish that you could go to sleep, there right in front of you is Jesus on the cross, the crucifix, with its crown of thorns and spear wounds, complete with the nails in His hands and feet.

The question comes to your mind a million times. What is this about? Many Christians today criticize this church for having Jesus on the cross. I am so thankful that they do. With Jesus in front of you on the cross it helps you to remember that relationship with God came to us through suffering. I am a Jesus man today because of it.

So there I was with Bryan, about to pray. It had been years since I was in the church of my youth. He had me kneel down, bow my head and close my eyes. I did it and then he had me repeat after him. "I confess that I am a sinner, that I want to be forgiven." The most important part, "if You are there Jesus, if You are real, I will follow You." After twenty seconds we were done. I was thinking it cannot be over this quick, yet I said amen and I opened my eyes.

The result was that the world was a different place, when I went outside the air felt different, green leaves were greener, life had a different texture. I felt light as a feather and later found out that since my sin was removed, that is why I felt lighter, I was stunned.

People were trying to get to me, my brother was trying to talk to me. I still could not stand Christians and they were all around me. Thank the Lord, my brother backed off. It was like I had come out of a dream and was on a different planet. A planet where God was real. People were still a pain but God was real and He had shown Himself to me.

I went home and started telling everyone that He was real. The people from my old church did not want to talk to me so I went to the highway and byways. I hitch hiked up and down the freeways just to get in people's cars and tell them that He was real. They could know Him, many would ask how? I told them that if they would pray with me for twenty seconds, He would let them know He was there. Many of these people would pull off of the road and cry. They would say things like "I never knew."

I would go to the lake near my home and point at the beauty that surrounded us, I would tell people that God had placed that natural beauty there because He loved them and if they would pray with me they could know Him.

People would hear me talking and come over to identify themselves as Christians. I would get away as fast as I could.

My brother would come around sometimes and tell me that I needed to find a church, "you need fellowship" he would say. When I got alone with the Lord I would say that I really loved spending time with Him but please don't tell me Lord that You want me to join a church.

I also would go to parties and smoke pot, drink and cuss while I told everybody that "He is real."

Christians were always saying that they heard God's voice. I never had and I would talk all day to Him about this. Then one day it happened. I was sitting and just loving His presence. I had just finished the last joint or marijuana cigarette that I had. Then the Lord spoke to me, He said "you don't need that any more," I never had another.

He spoke to me on four occasions in the same manner. I would return to this place to hear His voice as though it were the place that was special. I guess it was special because it caused faith in me that if I was there He would speak to me. It is to this day "the place of my visitation" likes Moses' burning bush.

I began to hear His voice more often. One day He told me that I needed fellowship. He did not use the 'C' word though, you know, 'Church.' A girl from high school heard that I was religious and preaching every day at the lake. She came and found me to see if I wanted to go to some concerts with her. I had wondered if there were any more of those concerts, so I went with her. As we arrived at this concert venue another girl from high school who had tried to witness to me was yelling my name across the parking lot. She yelled, "Steve Orsillo what are you doing here?" You see, I had been particularly mean to her when she tried to tell me that "God loved me and wanted to know me." He had been answering me all along. You remember my questions about this cross while I was growing up. He had sent people like this girl to me to try an answer my questions. She had prayed for me back then and here I was. She really did not believe that her prayer was going to be answered. She asked if I belonged to a church. I told her what I thought, I guess she was used to that with me. It did not faze her. She invited me to a home group. I went, it was awesome.

We would worship acapella for hours with no leader. Just love songs to Jesus. I had never seen anything like this before. We all had to go to work in the morning yet we could never stop. Someone would eventually say "do you know that it is midnight?" We would all scatter looking for our shoes and belongings and flee home to sleep before work.

These young people were talking about going to a church. It did not take long for me to be seduced and I went with them. In a very short time I became the youth pastor at this church. My life in ministry began.

Being this new creature in Christ that was promised, was easy. Jesus was real and I followed Him. He led me to church, He led me to a righteousness that was good, not a burden at all. He has led me to grow up into a mature Christian and told me that I was responsible for how others perceive Him. I have followed Jesus for 34 years and He has led me where I did not want to go. I have been so poor that I had to pray for a dollar to put gas in my car to go to church. I have been very well off to make giving money away as the ministry that I operated. I also have been bankrupt. When I consider all of the roads that following Jesus has caused me to walk in, I have no regrets.

I was so lost, now I am found. I was so blind, now I see. Thirty four years of what some would call a fairy tale existence that I would not trade for anything in the world.

I did not trust God and He did not reject me. I hated His people and He did not forsake me. I had prayed as a child and He heard me. He got to me through all the emotion. I had totally rejected His church, His bride, and this did not intimidate Him.

For several years I went to this home group and was at this church for part of that time until I moved to the concert church in Sacramento. I had also begun my career in construction.

But I was growing lonely. I would plead with God for the love that I saw in marriage. When I had dreams about being married they would always be the same. In these dreams I would walk up the sidewalk leading to a home, I would open the back door which led to the kitchen and there was a woman standing there with her back to me, as she would turn around so that I could see her, it would be Vicki LaSorella.

Chapter 16

THE NEW VICKI

I HAD written Vicki about Jesus as soon as I had met Him. Her experience with the church we grew up in was not as negative as mine. It was just negative enough that she didn't want to go back to it and just positive enough to use it as a shield against what I was telling her. Really, she just thought that I was wearing pink togas and selling flowers in airports. Vicki also was in a long term relationship and it was not easy to think about me or anything that I was doing. Since I knew that I must not be "unequally yoked," I would not be able to have Vicki as my wife.

One day a friend heard that my construction job had been shut down for two weeks. He asked me if I could help him move to Seattle, Washington. I thought, Vicki is in Washington. I had just had another dream. I was beginning to have impure thoughts about Vicki. I made my plans. I would go to Seattle and try to seduce Vicki and get her away from this dude, lead her to Jesus, then repent, marry her and there you go. It is God's plan He keeps showing me in a dream so I will help it along a little.

When I got to Seattle where I was unloading this U-haul truck I had a file cabinet on my hand truck when the Lord spoke to me. "If you do what you have planned, you will never be able to say that you made it to marriage, you will never be able to have a testimony about this." He was telling me that you can not un-ring a bell or give back what you have stolen from Vicki. I placed my head on the file cabinet and began to cry. I told Him that I would not go to Spokane, I will go back home.

He said, "you can go to Spokane, but if you sow to the flesh, you will reap the flesh," (I would get Vicki). "If you go to Spokane and sow to the Spirit I will give you a spiritual harvest." I thought about it for only a second and knew that I would go to Spokane and I would sow only to the Spirit.

When I got off of the train in Spokane, I went to the same cousin's house that Vicki and I were both related to, it was her aunt's house who had been married to my uncle all of my life, that made her my aunt as well. She told me where Vicki lived so I borrowed my cousin's motorcycle and went to Vicki's house. When I approached the house I popped a wheelie into her front lawn. Vicki's friend was looking out of the window and was shocked to see a guy fly into the front lawn like a nut. Vicki answered the front door. It was as if I was in a time machine. We were as thick as thieves in seconds. I had been reunited with my best friend again.

God had said "sow to the Spirit." So, I held my distance, my eyes cast to the floor and I don't mind admitting that it was tough. It was hubba, hubba, ding, ding, this baby has everything. She was everything I remembered, so easy to talk to, so easy to be friends with and gorgeous as well. We spent all her spare time together, and so that I could keep my promise to sow only to the Spirit, all that I would talk about was Jesus. On just the second day I challenged her to pray with me for twenty seconds to find out if He is real. I would tell her I knew that when she was young and sitting in church she had questions about God and He had sent me to bring her the answers. I challenged her to pray with me for twenty seconds and talk to God. She took the challenge on May 1st, 1979 on the couch of our uncle's house, she prayed a twenty second prayer with me, just like the one that Bryan had prayed with me. God was suddenly real to her just like he had become real to me. She said that the world had changed. She was different and the world was different. God loved her and had forgiven her because of the cross and those wounds of His. What she had wondered and asked was answered. Vicki Lasorella was born again.

She went through the next day in awe and wonder. The world and all that was in it made sense. She was already telling everyone. She knew nothing of doctrine or religions. Just that He was real and you could know Him. I stood back not wanting to interfere with what she was feeling. I wanted her to know Him and not be confused about her feelings for me.

Eventually the inevitable was going to happen. I asked the Lord what to do and He showed me what to do. I really liked her, so then I kissed her. It was awesome. It had been five years waiting for my next chance to kiss Vicki. It was not sowing to the flesh, it was true love and it was nurtured by years of God's spiritual blessing. It was innocence and purity of affection that I had not even known was possible. We fell in love all over again and we decided that week that we should get married. I had to go back to California and finish my job. I was gone for about thirty days.

Vicki and I had decided that I would move up to Spokane and the day of my departure was planned. Little did I know that her ex-boyfriend came back to see her and really liked this Christian Vicki. She did not tell me, she just got confused.

I was supposed to leave to return to Spokane on Monday. I was at my parent's house on Saturday night to have dinner and say goodbye, when all of a sudden the Lord said as clearly as possible "get up and go now." To which I answered that it was late and I should be getting home. The Lord said "get up and go to Spokane now." So, I told my parents that I was leaving tonight to go to Spokane. I left and went to pack my van and by 1:00 am I was on the road. 21 hours later at 10:00 pm that night I had to stop and sleep. I called Vicki, who was not surprised that I was on the road early. She acted very strange about it. I hung up feeling more insecure than I had ever felt in my life. You see, Vicki had decided to change her mind, she called down to my mother to see if I was there and my mother told her that I was on the road. Vicki was freaking out and could not tell me on the phone. Vicki's mom offered to pay her way out of town before I arrived.

When I arrived in Spokane I went straight to Vicki's house. She soon came home from the college where she attended classes, when Vicki saw me she knew immediately that I was the one for her and she ran to my arms, the confusion was gone.

That was 30 years ago this month. We were married about one month later. We have followed the Lord together for thirty years. We "followed Him" and responded to His voice or we may have missed the fairy tale like life that He had in store for us. Thank God that He usually only shows you what you need to know for the moment.

Vicki Orsillo; as she later became known, is like the disciples of the Bible. She just went and told what Jesus had done for her. People listened and came to the Master to hear and see for themselves what He was like.

When we pastored youth or singles Vicki was the flavor that drew them in. Her faith would rival that of every kahuna in the land. She has forsaken all to "follow Him." She picks up her cross daily to give life and joy to everyone who comes.

As a mother Vicki has four children of her own not to mention many, many adopted children of this world. When they were look-ing for someone to love them they found Vicki and she led them to the Lord.

When one of our children was born with Down's Syndrome she did not miss a beat. "This one just needs more love" she said. That son Mark could have been born to anyone but he was born to Vicki Orsillo and let me tell you, he won the lottery of the womb on that one. We took it in stride, this was the road that God had given us, this is the gift that He prepared for us. To see Vicki on the floor stimulating that boy hour after hour always with love that only a mother can give. She was so gifted at mothering that she could take care of a medically and physically challenged baby and never neglect Colie our beautiful daughter.

It was Vicki that God spoke to when Mark was aspirating and was near death, back in his bedroom. The Lord said to Vicki while she was cleaning up the kitchen, "go check on that boy." She dropped what she was doing and ran to his room. He was near death, any delay would have been fatal. It was Vicki who directed me to drive to the fire station instead of the hospital. The firemen saved Mark's life. The hospital would have been too far.

Mark would not be with us today had she not learned to listen to the voice of the Lord and followed Him.

Vicki has become a Pastor at The Father's House Church. She prays with people who have been enslaved by the wounds of their past. To do this she has to hear the voice of the Lord. The Lord tells people what it is that is holding them hostage, then sets them free if they yield to His direction. She hears His voice and helps them get the healing that they need. People beg her for time slots. Some, who have paid many thousands of dollars for therapy have told Vicki that they get more freedom from spending time with her than they do with the paid professionals. She does not counsel, she just listens to God.

She has four children, all of them raised and out of the house. Mark is under the house in his own apartment and comes upstairs about thirty times each night. But he has his own address and so that makes our home an empty nest. Her children adore her and they know that they have been well loved and well mothered.

Her husband (me) can tell you that he also won the lottery of matrimony when she chose him over old what's-his-name. It's as if I have lived in a fairy tale. I have never known anyone to be more happily married than we have been. Sometimes Vicki wants to make a couple feel good who are struggling so she says, "yeah we had a bad year in our."...then she looks at me for help and I have to say that I don't know what she is talking about. We have not had a bad year, or month. I still would rather be with her than any person alive and when we play Marco Polo in the pool, I still cheat and make no apologies about it.

Vicki has decided to be a disciple and she has never ever turned back. I was there on May 1st, 1979 and was a witness to her meeting Jesus for the first time. He said come on Vicki "follow Me," she left everything and did just that. No turning back, not for money that we need today or money that we need for tomorrow. She is a disciple of Jesus, a follower. Vicki is Christian and has a place in heaven.

She won't be going alone, Vicki understands that as you grow in the Lord and gain in faith and stature that it is not intended that you get there alone. She tells those that God has placed in her life, "follow me as I follow Christ and I won't lead you astray."

It takes a special commitment and a special person to take someone who is wandering and floundering up under your wing. Then tell them "stick with me I know the way out of this mess" and Vicki raises up countless young people, watching over them knowing that there are no robot disciples, everyone has a choice. As the one who will give her word "I will see you through," she mothers them all for her Jesus whom she has loved without wavering for thirty years.

I am reminded of Sam Gamgee the Hobbit when he said that the Lady Galadriel had told him "don't you leave him Sam Gamgee, don't you leave him." Sam would not leave him either. Sam was speaking of his master Frodo and he went all the way through many hells and beyond to keep his commitment.

That is how Vicki has served the Lord all of my life with her. Don't you leave Him Vicki, don't you leave Him. Vicki has not left Him either.

Just as the Lord called these men to leave all and "follow Me." Vicki heard His call and answered, Vicki has followed Jesus.

Jesus said, "*You are my disciple if you do what I have commanded you,*" Vicki my wife has definitely done this. Everyone who knows her feels loved by her. She has forsaken wealth and home, loved God more than all else.

We moved from Vicki's family in Spokane when the Lord had told me that it was time to leave Washington and returned to California. I said to the Lord that it would be nice if He could tell Vicki. One night not too long after I had said this to the Lord, I was reading in bed when Vicki sat up and declared, "God is sending us to California." I said "thank you Jesus." We put our house up for sale by putting a sign on the column in the front yard. A few hours later there was a knock on the door. It was a lady and she told me that she had wanted this house since she was a little girl. She bought it in the worst housing market that you could imagine.

We were on our way to California, where we lived and loved Jesus. Doing ministry and having more babies while we just enjoyed the life that comes when you hear His voice and hear Him tell you that He loves you as He calls you to "follow Me."

Chapter 17

3 I FLAVORS

THE VOICE of God's love and the call to come and "follow Him"
can become distant in the ministry when you deal with religion and
churches with many personalities. There are so many doctrinal differences and opinions, stresses and obligations. My call came at a time
when I was believing that there should be one way to serve Him and
was judging anyone who did it different. "Just follow the Word" I
would say. The problem, that I grew to understand was that people
got different messages from the Word. People heard different things
from the voice of God. Was one wrong and the other right? Then was
one type of music right and the other one wrong?

I had wondered about that when I was a young Christian. Jesus
seems to be having a hard time getting through to these people. I
know that I hear Him, how come they can't? All He is saying, after
all, is "follow Me."

The answer came one day when the Lord sat me down. He said
that I should consider that church was a lot like 31 flavors of ice

cream, some people like rocky road and some people like vanilla. The only reason for a flavor of ice cream to be in the store is that someone wants it. That is why it is offered.

The Lord said that Christian 'following' was based on giving people the desires of their hearts. Drawing people to what they like. For instance, moths like flames, then if moths got saved there would need to be the fire church. Some people like hymn music, some like contemporary music, still others no music at all. In the same way some people like shouters and others like rhymers. What works to draw one does not work to draw another. The fact that there are so many different ideas may just be God's plan.

As we complain and struggle against these differences and try to bring a unity that is described as all of us doing the same things, ringing the same bell, sounding the same and looking the same, we may find ourselves opposing God.

There is a group of people who vocally criticize the "seeker sensitive" movement. Now when I talk to people who work in "seeker sensitive" churches they tend to almost apologize for the word and lower their voice as they say it. My experience with these churches is that they preach Jesus and teach Christian living to more people than any other group in the west. The most well known of these leaders is Rick Warren. If you hear him on television you know that he loves the Lord and is not shy about Jesus and His teachings at all. I have gone to many of these so called "seeker sensitive" churches, some have forgotten who Jesus is and have turned the message into a positive mental attitude seminar. The majority like Cornerstone in Chandler, Arizona and Life Center in Spokane, Washington are straight forward Jesus churches with the message of the cross and the message that Jesus gave His best for you, have you given your best for Him?

Maybe "seeker sensitive" would "not be your cup of tea" and Pentecostal just "does not sit well with you." How about a nice denominational church or ecumenical church for you then? Whatever you want, I have great news for you, God has these and a lot more. I bet He has something for everyone. He probably wishes that we would stop throwing stones at each other. Is the absence of stone throwing what He calls unity? I believe unity is defined by the fact that we support each other by accepting each other's faith as valid, and that we stop verbally throwing stones at one another. Only those who have not stumbled around in ministry and made mistakes, those who have never done it wrong, should throw the stones. I guess that I should quote my good friend Jesus here and say that "whoever has not sinned, let him throw the first stone." Is that what unity would look like? If we stopped criticizing one another, being jealous of each other, picking at one another.

Some of the most horrible things that I see blogged on the internet these days is Christian on Christian bantering back and forth. The terrible name calling, and mistrust that we have for the things that make us uncomfortable are all over the net. Things that we have decided are unscriptural, the doctrinal positions that we take. We criticize each other for the way that we live out the calling of God in our lives. Yet each one of us will face judgement one day for the way that we responded to only one thing, the words of Jesus. Did we do what He told us to do? Did we believe in the Lord Jesus Christ? Did we love each other?

If any person hears the call of the Lord to leave all and "follow Me," then if I feel a similar call and want to join that person in the work of the ministry of Jesus, I should simply look and see if there is any fruitfulness in what they are doing and how they are doing it, their methods. I should determine my position on what they are doing based solely on the fruitfulness of the venture, asking myself if this is the ministry of Jesus and can I add to the fruit? If I add myself as an ingredient to this venture, then just maybe we will have created a new flavor in the Kingdom of God. Instead of being critical of the fact that there are thousands of different expressions of the Christian experience, we can rejoice that there is yet another way for people to come to Jesus and be saved. We can be excited that "Jesus is preached and in this we rejoice."

Some say that if Christ is real and the Christian church wants to be seriously relevant, that we should all get together and do it as one. Doing "it" as one would be nice, but I am sure that the arguments of what that would look like would cause us all to quit doing the good that we were doing just to try to get together to do "it" together.

One pastor that I knew said that he would not do anything until we all do "it" together. I said that it was a pretty sure thing that He would not be doing anything in the near future. We had many good talks about these ideas. I would use military metaphors and say that the Army should do what the Army does and the Navy what the Navy does. My motive was to get his very giftedness into action in the city that God had given to us.

A radio preacher that I knew said that if us Christians were serious about being relevant, then we should quit meeting in all of these different churches and rent one big convention center to meet in. "One church" was what he was describing. He said that any other idea was not the love that God wanted. The next time we met I asked him about this. I asked if he would imagine this "one church" and try to come to a conclusion about the music and the style of teaching, the way that the service would flow, the length of the service. Many more details would have to be worked out but when once you had come to a conclusion, you would have one church in your city. There would be one type of music, one type of teaching, one style of everything. Only those people who liked those types would have a church. The question would have to be asked, if in a few months would there be more fruit or less fruit? You could not know for sure but you could guess that it would be less. The city that God gave to His people, all of His people, would have only one style, one message, one set of leaders.

I asked my friend, the man who thought this would work, then why is there not only one sport, or one television choice each night? How come if this "one choice" idea was for the church, how come it didn't work in all aspects of life? How about the different shapes of people? The different looks of clothing?

The television show Star Trek back in the 60's and 70's, when they visited a planet everybody looked the same. Where and in what imagination does everybody dress the same and like the same things. If you found this planet, wouldn't it be a boring planet to live on? A planet where everyone was the same wouldn't be earth, and it wouldn't be America.

So many people want to believe that we are all the same. We are not all the same so why should the church only cater to those who are the same. There really should be those that "quake" and those that "shake." Those who dress in suits and ties and those who come as they are. Does one or the other have to be wrong? Or could there really be 31 flavors and many more. Could it really be okay to have music and a style for every taste?

It is clear that we must find a way to be unified. Unified in a way that celebrates our differences and keeps the integrity of the command of Jesus to "love one another as He has loved us."

A good place to start is by not verbally attacking each other. It would be important that we not criticize each other for the choices that are not immoral or destructive to others.

I think it would be good to include an understanding of the fact that it is a good thing that we are different and we present different ways and styles. That we do "it" different to attract and feed spiritually a much more diverse group of people. I believe that 31 types of churches is far short of the plan that God has to present the message of Jesus to His world. God made us different and He gave us different tastes, styles and languages so let us continue to expand the flavors of the church until we have "preached the gospel to every nation, tongue and people."

Chapter 18

HOW DID WE
GET HERE?

IN 1986, I had a particularly tough time in the ministry and decided to get my contractor's license. I had been in construction since I was 18 years old and I had been doing ministry since 19. In 1986 I was 30 years old and had my third child. I had been a foreman on most jobs and worked it around my ministry for many years. Since it became evident that owning my own business was going to be better pay and more flexible time constraints, I started Steve Orsillo Construction and as Forest Gump said, "God showed up." We were blessed, we for the first time had money in the bank.

The ministry on the other hand was painful and I was surely suffering. So I sat out, it would only be for a season but I said, "if the Lord calls me I will come." He had lost my number or so I had thought. I focused my love for God on giving and my business on leading trades people to Jesus, business was good.

One day He called, we were moving and did not know where. In my business I had invested in a house in Oroville. The Gulf war began and this house would not sell, it was on a incredible 5 acres with a view to the ends of the earth, you could almost see heaven from there.

We discussed Oroville as the city of our destiny but I had said these words to my wife, "the last place that I want to move is Oroville, I have played baseball up there all my life and it is a horrible town." I proceeded to drive to Oroville to check on that house which is about an hour and a half drive. When I came to the driveway to the house the Lord spoke to me. He said, "this is where I have you and this is what I have for you, Oroville." Atfirst I said, "yes Lord this is all that I have ever wanted, just to know your will." Then I said, "you're going to have to tell Vicki because I just told her how bad Oroville is." I called her and asked, "did the Lord speak to you since I left," she answered, "He said were moving to Oroville." She rented the U-Haul truck as I drove home, and we proceeded to load up and move to Oroville, California. We arrived at 1:00 am. The next morning I unloaded and we were living in Oroville by mid September of 1991. The next thing that I said to the Lord was, "Ok we are here, what are we here for?"

Vicki and I had always "followed Him." Jesus came to me in Stockton, California and He showed me that He was real so I dropped all (which wasn't much) and "followed Him." Vicki had heard and felt the Lord in Spokane, Washington then she dropped all and "followed Him." We had heard Him and followed the Bread of Life crumbs to our marriage. We had heard Him say "go to California" and we moved. We had "sowed to the spirit" because we believed that He had promised us something and taught us truths.

When we were in California, we continued to "follow Him" until He told us that He had Oroville for us. We had learned over a period of many years to "go" where Jesus sends us, and to come where He calls us.

The call of God in our lives is to us the will of God. Jesus lets us know in many ways what it is that He wants us to do. One way He speaks is to the heart of man and Vicki and I have learned to trust the 'voice' of God. Following His voice we have believed many wonderful things and have trusted for our lives. We have trusted for The Father's House Church, we have seen countless lives touched and enriched by the work of this church.

We have started and operated Steve Orsillo Construction by this voice of God. Trusted for the knowledge of how to operate it as a partner or provider to a church. The knowledge of how to work two full time jobs for many years and not burn out. All while you enjoy your family, loving your spouse, with your children being part of everything you do. God knows how and if we listen to Him we will succeed, at least in His definition of success.

Vicki and I have pinched ourselves to see if it is all real. Can our lives be this blessed and we ask ourselves, how did we get here? What are the building blocks of a life so satisfying and fulfilling? What did we do to get here is the question that I ask God, as I see it Vicki and I only did a few things right. We did a little bit more right than wrong, stumbling along just trying to keep our priorities right. What we learned as we went is the definition of the call of Jesus to "follow Me," It does mean to follow that voice that tells you to "move here" or "go there." To follow also means read His Word the Bible and do what God has said to do. I think that people really confuse it here.

It is sometimes a crutch to say that "God said," when someone wants to use "God said" as an excuse to do what they want to do. I just make sure that what He is saying to me or to them does not confuse what He has already said. Since the phrase "God said" is easily misused, I must weigh what I hear against the Bible and my understanding of scripture. His word the Bible is very direct, and I believe very simple. Then, I must have confidential wise counsel that I reveal my "words from the Lord" to and I ask them if they agree. These people must have proven track records for me and then if they agree, the "God said" becomes God's will and this is then the call of God on our lives.

I also must have the wisdom as a leader to learn which voices are

God's and which ones are not His voice. The wise counsel is the confirmation I use to learn these lessons. In everyone's life there will be the call of God that does not allow time or opportunity to confirm His will and when this happens in my life I want to know that I can trust in God. When He gives me an assignment and I am under the authority of someone else, or in partnership with another, like my wife or when I am on a church staff, where I am under the pastor or church council, then I must trust their ability to hear Him and trust their willingness to follow. The trusting God part is in His ability to convince them if He wants me to do something. He has been one hundred percent successful in my experience. God does not seem intimidated by these obstacles and He seems very willing to help those of us who want to get it right when following Him.

Every once in a while a leader in my church will tell me that "God said," just before they tell me that He said something that is probably wrong or not going to work out very well for them, it could be a subject like what God wants the church to do. Then, after I tell them that I don't agree they say, "I have to listen to God not man." When I trust the person I will let them know that what they are saying contradicts how they quoted what He said in the past. Or I may have to let them know the pattern of their life is to follow their own counsel and ask them if doing this has worked out well in the past. I ask, "what does the fruit of these past decisions look like?"

One young lady was in a marital catastrophe and clinging to my every advice while she sought the Lord for His peace. During this time a man who was not pleased with the advice I had been giving her, gave her some advice. He told her that she should not be listening to man she should be listening to God, the man he was talking about was me. She answered him and said, "God put Steve in my life as my pastor and he does help me hear God, God told me to listen to Steve."

This young lady did not expect to have this catastrophe in her life, this day to day pain was not what she had expected when she went to an altar and was joined to her husband. What she did not need was someone adding to that pain by trying to take her confidence in her wise counsel away. What was very rewarding to me and to this couple who are doing great, ministering in church, receiving mentoring, was the reason they listened to me. They said, "we have seen the fruit of your life and decided that you know the way. We looked at the fruit of those others who wanted to give us advice and the fruit of their lives was destruction and decay." These two had heard me when they weren't in trouble, they had read the new testament and listen to the sermons on inspecting the fruit and watching out for stumbling blocks. They had learned in advance how confusing it can be to try and hear clearly the instructions of the Lord when you are in gut wrenching turmoil, you need trust worthy people who know God and hear Him. You must inspect the fruit and trust the fruit in advance because trying to figure it out on the run in the middle of the trials is very hard and not very reliable.

It is easier when the Bible is clearly telling me what to do, especially when it is the words of Jesus in the gospels or the Book of Revelation. Yet the Bible has been used to pervert more teaching and cause more confusion than any other source that I can think of. One thing that I have done that is probably the best answer to my question to myself of "how did we get here," is that I pray continually, or at least on an everyday basis this prayer to God, "heal my wrong thinking and teach me your ways, show me your path, lead me in the way that is righteousness and let me not be led astray, let me honor You in all of my ways that I might not sin against You." I have prayed this or something very similar for all of my Christian days, and I would give this practice of praying to be unconfused and led to the truth as the best answer for the question "how did we get here." He has led us here in answer to our prayers, our faith has been in Him!

Chapter 19

LISTEN TO JESUS

WHAT I have done is learned a very important lesson at a very young Christian age. I was given a book by Andrew Murray called "With Christ in the School of Prayer." This is a most phenomenal book and the content is without compare. In this book Murray teaches that the power in prayer comes from the relationship that you have with God. Yet it is the title that has changed my life more than any single written word outside the Bible has ever come close to.

The brilliance of this idea is that we should have Jesus be our teacher on any subject. It is the most simple basic idea that I have ever heard to this day.

With Christ in the School of any subject seems to me to be the easiest way to get it right, no matter what you are trying to get right. With Christ as your teacher in the school of obedience, giving, loving, abiding in the vine, and just plain living the principles of the Word of God. Having Jesus be your teacher is the simplest way to come to a point in your life where you say to yourself, how did I get so blessed?

The Bible is full of really good and interesting stories. But, it has two basic things that anyone should know who is going to try to "follow Jesus."

There is a Old Covenant and a New Covenant. They are called the Old Testament and the New Testament. They teach us about the life of being God's people under each covenant.

The Old Covenant was known as the Law and the Prophets. People lived under the Law, and these Prophets told them what God was saying. Sin was not forgiven very easily yet a person could have their sins forborne to the future by the sacrifice of a lamb. The blood shed of this lamb would appease the need for payment for your sins. It was like a big bulldozer would shove your sins into the future to be paid for at a later date.

The New Covenant was the promise to the people who followed the Old Covenant that things were going to change. One of the changes that was coming was that a man was going to be born to them and He would be known as "Immanuel" or "God is with us." He would be the Messiah, the Christ, the Son of the Living God. He would be the sacrifice for our sins. The difference being, He would be the "Lamb of God who takes away the sins of the world." Not forbearing them any longer but removing them.

In this new Covenant, there was a wonderful new result, if a man could be forgiven then he could be Holy and Righteous. Man could qualify to have interaction with God. Man could walk with Him and talk with Him, laugh with Him and cry with Him, not just priests and prophets but the every day common man. If this would happen then a man could actually become the dwelling place of God's Holy Spirit. The Temple of the Living God. God even said that after this happened He would no longer live in temples made by the hands of man. He would live in the hearts of men and women who loved Him. This would be a new day and a new way. God was coming to every man and giving every man the chance to be forgiven and to know Him.

God would now give every man a chance to become His sons and daughters. Not a chance, like a race, a game or a match where one wins and one loses or one wins and everybody else loses. In this race everyone who runs wins, *"the first will be last and the last will be first."* Everyone who goes after the prize gets it. The prize is this, *"to everyone who believes He gave the power to become children of God."*

In the Old Covenant, the people who followed God rarely called Him "Father." In the New Covenant, Jesus the Messiah who is described as "God with us" said that He came to reveal the Father. Jesus said that "He only did what the Father told Him to do, He only said what the Father told Him to say." Jesus came to show us God as our Father and to give us the chance to "become the children of God." In teaching us to pray Jesus started with telling us to pray this "Our Father." As much as I love the Old Covenant and all of the wonderful stories of David and Solomon, of Moses and Abraham, they could not be "sons of God" nor did they call the King of Heaven and Lord over all of the earth, their Father. To follow their teachings is like shooting for the bottom rung of the ladder. If that is as high as you want to get, then go for it. Men did that for thousands of years. They did not achieve sonship or have access to the throne room of God.

Jesus came to cause us to be "born again" as sons and daughters of "Our Father who is in Heaven." Let's say that I have one or two hours out of twenty four that is mine each day, to study the subject of how I should then live and what I, as a leader should teach people. If this short time is what I have, then how should I use it? Should I use it to study what someone say like Solomon who could only bemoan the fact that he did not know God well enough would say who only achieved the status of servant or slave? Or should I use this time to study Jesus, who claimed that He was the Son of God and "He was going to prepare a place for us" in His Father's house? He promised He would fill us with the Holy Spirit and "take away the sins of the world" which includes my sins. Should I listen to Jesus, more than any other? Now put down your stones you don't have to stone me, I love the revelations of the Old Covenant, I am so very fortunate to live in the days after the invention of the printing press so that I have easy access to the whole Word of God.

This "listen to Jesus" idea was not my idea. We have two others that we can credit this idea to. Jesus took several of His disciples up on a mountain. We call this mountain the Mount of transfiguration. When they get up there, Moses and Elijah met them there and talk to Jesus. Peter, who has followed the Law and the Prophets all of his life said, "*Lord, it is good for us to be here; if You wish, I will make three tabernacles here, one for You, and one for Moses, and one for Elijah. While he was still speaking, a bright cloud overshadowed them, and behold, a voice out of the cloud said, This is My beloved Son, with whom I am well-pleased; listen to Him!*"

The Father says that we should "listen to Him" (Jesus that is). In addition to this, Jesus says in John chapter 12 that "His" words will judge us in the end. Two very reliable witnesses that testify undeniably that we should "listen to Him."

I have conducted a very unscientific study of the contemporary Christian teachings of our days and the conclusion that I have come to is that we have chosen to not "listen to Him." What I have done is paid attention to the sermons that I hear people giving on the radio and at conferences, not to mention the guest speakers at my church. Very few are messages on the teachings of Jesus, about eight in ten are from and about verses in the Old Testament, great stories about God and how He interacted with the children of Israel. Almost none of the sermons that I have been hearing are on the verses found in the New Covenant and teach the words of Jesus, words that the Father of Heaven said that we should "listen to." Words that would help us to become the "children of God," as opposed to becoming the "children of Israel." The very words that Jesus said would judge us in the end.

It seems to me that it would be important to major on the teachings of Jesus. Doing so will cost a person a great deal. To "love your enemy and do good to those who persecute you," expensive! To "give to anyone who asks of you," difficult! Not to mention that, "laying down your life for your brother," "picking up your cross" and "loving one another as I have loved you" will cost us our lives.

Jesus said that you "*saw Me hungry and you did not feed Me.*"

When the disciples were confronted with diseases they were expected to heal them, when it was demons they were asked why they did not cast it out. In a storm when they were afraid and they did not calm the storm they were rebuked. Peter saw Jesus walk on water and said to Jesus, *"Lord, if it is You, command me to come to You on the water."* Jesus answered *"come."* When Peter sank, it was obvious from what Jesus said that sinking was not what was expected.

Jesus told the disciples *"Go therefore and make disciples of all the nations, baptizing them in the name of the Father and the Son and the Holy Spirit, teaching them to observe all that I commanded you; and lo, I am with you always, even to the end of the age." "Go into all the world and preach the Gospel to every nation."*

Do we really need to find other things to teach, have we really finished with even the basics yet? When you see one of the least of these my brothers hungry and you do not feed them you have not fed Jesus.

" Listen to Him," read Matthew 25: 31-46

"But when the Son of Man comes in His glory, and all the angels with Him, then He will sit on His glorious throne. All the nations will be gathered before Him; and He will separate them from one another, as the shepherd separates the sheep from the goats; and He will put the sheep on His right, and the goats on the left. Then the King will say to those on His right, "Come, you who are blessed of My Father, inherit the kingdom prepared for you from the foundation of the world. For I was hungry, and you gave Me something to eat; I was thirsty, and you gave Me something to drink; I was a stranger, and you invited Me in; naked, and you clothed Me; I was sick, and you visited Me; I was in prison, and you came to Me." Then the righteous will answer Him, "Lord, when did we see You hungry, and feed You, or thirsty, and give You something to drink? And when did we see You a stranger, and invite You in, or naked, and clothe You? When did we see You sick, or in prison, and come to You?" The King will answer and say to them, "Truly I say to you, to the extent that you did it to one of these brothers of Mine, even the least of them, you did it to Me." Then He will also say to those on His left, "Depart from

Me, accursed ones, into the eternal fire which has been prepared for the devil and his angels; for I was hungry, and you gave Me nothing to eat; I was thirsty, and you gave Me nothing to drink; I was a stranger, and you did not invite Me in; naked, and you did not clothe Me; sick, and in prison, and you did not visit Me." Then they themselves also will answer, "Lord, when did we see You hungry, or thirsty, or a stranger, or naked, or sick, or in prison, and did not take care of You?" Then He will answer them, "Truly I say to you, to the extent that you did not do it to one of the least of these, you did not do it to Me. These will go away into eternal punishment, but the righteous into eternal life."

Eternal punishment? Eternal life? Accursed ones! Eternal fires! This is serious stuff, and have we really graduated to any other subject than these most important words of Jesus? I have not even scratched the surface yet!

Consider the words of Jesus about "forgive and you will be forgiven, do not forgive and you will not be forgiven." "Listen to Him" the Father says!

I now see what the Apostle meant when he said to "work out your salvation with fear and trembling." The word "work" is probably the problem for most of us. We want this to be easy, but it wasn't for the Apostles. It wasn't for Jesus. Because he "listened to Him," Paul was whipped five times with the forty minus one for mercy, that is one hundred ninety five lashes with the whip in his lifetime. Shipwrecked, stoned and left for dead! Running from those who opposed the teaching of the words of Jesus. Paul listened to Jesus and it cost Paul his life. He was beheaded in a dirt hole of a prison just outside of Rome far from home and family. Jesus said *"if you don't love me more than mother, father, sister or brother, you cannot be my disciple."*

To answer the call of Jesus to "follow Me," it wasn't just the disciples and Apostles who had to forsake all and go into the whole world, and "love one another," risking their lives. This call is for every person who answers the call in their day and in all days, including today, "listening to Him," and doing what He calls us to do as His disciples.

The Father said "listen to Him" , Jesus said His words would be the judge of our lives. Jesus said the ones who receive eternal life would be the ones who fed Him, and Peter walked on water because He just obeyed and went. Jesus said the evidence of being His disciple is that we love each other as He has loved us. These and more are the call of Jesus on our lives, to do what He says and be salt to the world as His disciples, not trying to use Christianity as salt to flavor our lives.

Chapter 20

FOLLOW ME AND I WILL SHOW YOU THE WAY

PAUL WAS met by Jesus on the road. After this he was taught by the same Apostles that Jesus taught. He followed them in their teachings and submitted to them.

We get so much of our 'following' understanding from this amazing disciple and Apostle of Jesus. He said one thing that is so important to all of us. He said "*follow me as I follow Christ.*" Some translations say "*Imitate me as I imitate Christ.*" Jesus had told the Apostles to "*teach them all that I have commanded you.*" Jesus did not say, teach them to listen to My voice in the spirit and do only what I say. He told the Apostles to tell them themselves. Jesus said "*you will be My witnesses to the ends of the earth.*"

The stories of Paul and Peter alone tell us that these men expected other men to follow their lead. Paul the Apostle seems to have gotten mad when the teachings of Jesus were changed to excuse a life of sin. *"I wish that they would mutilate themselves,"* did he say that? The nature of these men who rise up to heroic stature after really struggling seems to shake them free of their former selves. Trying to bury the old man and be truly born again to new life, new self and a whole new way of serving the very Father God and Creator they had always served. I bet that the original eleven Apostles plus the guy chosen by the casting of lots would rather not say "follow me as I follow Christ" right after the whole deserting Jesus at the cross and then going fishing ordeal. I know when I have been confused or found out that my righteousness was not what I had hoped that it would be, I would rather not lead anyone or be an example to them either. Then Jesus pulls them all together and tells them *"you will be my witnesses to the ends of the earth." "Go therefore and make disciples of all the nations, baptizing them in the name of the Father and the Son and the Holy Spirit, teaching them to observe all that I commanded you."*

Big jobs don't you think? I can almost hear their thoughts ringing out over two thousand plus years right into my head. Did He forget what we just did? John records the conversation like this, Peter said *"Lord, You know all things; You know that I love You"* Jesus said to him, *"Tend My sheep."* In my paraphrase it goes like this, He answers them, "no you are just as I chose you, perfect for the job that I have prepared for you." You know when He tells Peter to *"feed My sheep"* it is as if He is saying to Him "I love you just the way that you are Peter, you are the one that I have chosen to feed My sheep." At least that is how I want to read it. You get the idea that Peter is about to say, "but I failed you," instead he says *"you know that I love you."* Jesus then does something so incredible, He says *"but when you grow old, you will stretch out your hands and someone else will gird you, and bring you where you do not wish to go. Now this He said, signifying by what kind of death he would glorify God. And when He had spoken this, He said to him, Follow Me!"* Jesus knows that Peter's failure is on Peter's mind and Peter thinks that this failure is what Jesus is thinking about also. I read it as Jesus saying "Peter you denied Me, but when you are old you are going to get another chance and then you will not fail." Jesus is telling Peter "you will glorify God!" but He is also telling him that he will be killed for his faith. We know the end of the story and Peter never held back or denied Christ again. What a man, I will follow him any day.

I love the story about the next time Peter is confronted by the rulers who accused Jesus and got Him crucified. It is in the book of Acts in the fourth chapter. It says, then Peter, filled with the Holy Spirit, said to them, "*Rulers and elders of the people, if we are on trial today for a benefit done to a sick man, as to how this man has been made well, let it be known to all of you and to all the people of Israel, that by the name of Jesus Christ the Nazarene, whom you crucified, whom God raised from the dead--by this name this man stands here before you in good health.*"

"*He is the STONE WHICH WAS REJECTED by you, THE BUILDERS, but WHICH BECAME THE CHIEF CORNER STONE. And there is salvation in no one else; for there is no other name under heaven that has been given among men by which we must be saved.*"

"*Now as they observed the confidence of Peter and John and understood that they were uneducated and untrained men, they were amazed, and began to recognize them as having been with Jesus. And seeing the man who had been healed standing with them, they had nothing to say in reply. But when they had ordered them to leave the Council, they began to confer with one another, saying, "What shall we do with these men? For the fact that a noteworthy miracle has taken place through them is apparent to all who live in Jerusalem, and we cannot deny it. But so that it will not spread any further among the people, let us warn them to speak no longer to any man in this name." And when they had summoned them, they commanded them not to speak or teach at all in the name of Jesus. But Peter and John answered and said to them, "Whether it is right in the sight of God to give heed to you rather than to God, you be the judge; for we cannot stop speaking about what we have seen and heard."*

Peter says *"Jesus Christ the Nazarene, whom you crucified."* I love this story, he says *"you be the judge;"* I think what Jesus said to Peter on that shore while they had breakfast really had an effect on Him and what better way to see it than to look at the next time His life was in danger. He tells them that they crucified the Messiah and *"He is the STONE WHICH WAS REJECTED by you, THE BUILDERS."* No pulled punches here, no fear, no denying Jesus here, it's have your way with me if you see fit. I am preaching His name and what I have seen and heard. Which does include what the rulers have done. If it was me in Peter's shoes I would be thinking, I won't fail you again Jesus.

When these heros of the faith, these chosen ones of Jesus, my brothers the Apostles say "imitate me as I imitate Christ" I am all in on that one.

These men did not leave a weak-kneed example to follow either. They were whipped and beaten, imprisoned and killed, stoned and left for dead. Some were shipwrecked and endured storms and persecution, having to run for their lives. One was boiled in oil and when he survived was exiled to a remote prison island. Stoned to death, run through with a sword, beheaded and crucified upside down, this was just some of the ways they were killed. After the resurrection of Jesus not one of them ran again or failed in his duty to Jesus to fulfill His commission of them.

They were faithful to the call of Jesus to "follow Me," they really did leave their homes and even all to "follow Him" and obey Him. They have loved me just as Jesus loved me, laying down their lives, they have written their letters and their stories for me to read, letters that I cherish for my life. Following them as they have followed Jesus before me has been one of the most rewarding experiences of my life. I will continue to answer the call of Jesus to "follow Me" and I will continue to follow these disciples as they have followed Jesus.

Chapter 21

AUTHORITY

A CENTURION sent friends to Jesus to ask Him to do something for him, his servant was sick and he came to Jesus for the solution. This Centurion was a Roman soldier and Centurion was his rank. In the Roman army, there were conquering armies and also there were occupying garrisons. It is believed that this Centurion was the leading sergeant of a garrison of Roman soldiers that was occupying Israel. It was said of him that he was a good man and had even helped the synagogue with their building.

This Centurion had heard of Jesus and knew where to go for help when a servant that he valued and loved became ill. He sent his Jewish friends to Jesus with the request that Jesus heal his servant.

In Luke 7 we read: *"When he heard about Jesus, he sent some Jewish elders asking Him to come and save the life of his slave. When they came to Jesus, they earnestly implored Him, saying, "He is worthy for You to grant this to him; for he loves our nation and it was he who built us our synagogue." Now Jesus started on His way with them;*

and when He was not far from the house, the Centurion sent friends, saying to Him, "Lord, do not trouble Yourself further, for I am not worthy for You to come under my roof; for this reason I did not even consider myself worthy to come to You, but just say the word, and my servant will be healed. For I also am a man placed under authority, with soldiers under me; and I say to this one, 'Go!' and he goes, and to another, 'Come!' and he comes, and to my slave, 'Do this!' and he does it." Now when Jesus heard this, He marveled at him, and turned and said to the crowd that was following Him, "I say to you, not even in Israel have I found such great faith." When those who had been sent returned to the house, they found the slave in good health."

Jesus says that this Roman gentile, a heathen from a Jewish perspective, had shown more excellent faith than anyone that He had seen in all of Israel. What had Jesus heard that was notable of such a declaration? All that the man said was that Jesus did not have to come to his house, and this Centurion said that he was a man under authority, he had men under him. He knew that Jesus did not have to come to his house, but instead Jesus only had to say the word and his servant would be healed. It was clearly not only the belief that Jesus could heal from a distance that was declared the greatest faith shown in all of Israel. It was also because the Centurion said I am a man under authority and I have people under my authority, so because of this fact, you can heal my servant. My paraphrase goes like this, I follow orders and people follow my orders so I know that if you (Jesus) give an order it will be carried out.

Is it possible that Jesus declares this the greatest statement of faith in all of Israel because it is the very building block of faith? Is it that knowing the identity of the Father, and His Son and the understanding of this by the person who is asking for the answer is the definition of faith? Does knowing that the Father's authority has been given to Jesus, and because of this, Jesus has power over demons and diseases, really qualify as the greatest statement of faith in all of Israel?

Does understanding that a man following orders and being someone who gives orders, expecting that they are followed, qualify as the description of "the essence of things hoped for, and the presence of things unseen" which is the biblical definition of faith? In other words, does being a man under authority and a man of authority give one the foundation for knowing that healing and power over sickness are a definite outcome? Jesus has this authority from His Father, since the Centurion expresses that he knows this, he can trust in the answer? No need for Jesus to come to his house. Jesus said it and because of his understanding of authority, the fact that Jesus said it, settles it, period!! I see here what Jesus meant when He made this statement about what the Centurion said. I believe that Jesus said this for our benefit, to teach us about being ruled and then ruling. This is about the definite outcome of the command of true authority.

If I am a man under authority, what does that look like? I believe that it describes a person who is answering the call of Jesus to "follow Me." It describes a person who does what Jesus says and then teaches others to follow Jesus by their example. This man would have a definite outcome, his behavior would be determined by the authority above him, definitely!

This requires that a person would take on the responsibility for their neighbor, even saying to their people and family "follow me as I follow Jesus" and I will not lead you astray.

Can you imagine if pastors would take on this calling to be responsible for the flock, understanding that their actions would cause others to stumble or help still others to make it through. I say to my congregation this phrase on a regular basis. "Follow me as I follow Jesus and I won't let you down. I am a man under the authority of the Father and I come in the name of Jesus." "Imitate me, follow me, get up next to me and do as I do." Then I make them a promise, "if you will do this for two years then at then end of this time you will like the changes in your life."

Many years ago I heard a pastor named Roy Hicks Jr. say that the responsibility of his congregation watching him and following him was on some days the only thing that kept him saved. Roy said that it made him a better man. It challenged him to step up to the calling in his life to be a light to the world, a leader.

If leaders only knew that if they move forward others are following and if they fall back, others are following that to.

We need in the Christian church everywhere to understand that someone is following us and that we are people under authority. We are either leading them to dominion over the diseases and demons or we are leading them to submission to demons, diseases and this world's system. What would happen in a church where everybody understood that someone is following them? That their example is being imitated by someone?

Chapter 22

BAIT

LUKE SAYS, "He (Jesus) said to His disciples, "It is inevitable that stumbling blocks come, but woe to him through whom they come! It would be better for him if a millstone were hung around his neck and he were thrown into the sea, than that he would cause one of these little ones to stumble."

Would parenting change if on each day, parents were aware that their children are imitating them? Would parents smoke if they could get their minds around the fact that 80% of children who grow up in households that smoke will end up smoking themselves?

Would Christians who have decided to drink alcohol in a public place do so at the risk of having millstones hung around their neck if someone who sees them employing their freedoms are caused to drink because they want that freedom also? With alcohol being so powerful and so destructive, is there any chance at all that the "strong, free, non-performance oriented Christian" who drinks in public has put a "stumbling block" in front of "one of these little ones?" I wonder if all of the discussion on this subject includes the "stumbling block" described as the word bait, as in the bait that is used in a trap. In Jesus' warning about us being one who baits someone, Jesus then says *"it would be better if a millstone were hung around his neck and he were thrown into the sea."* Jesus even used the word "woe," to describe an outcome that was worse than the "stone and sea." I wonder if the risk is worth it to the "little ones" or to the baiter.

At The Father's House we ask the people in attendance to raise their hands if they have ever felt enslaved by an addiction to a substance. Then we ask them to look around and see that they are not alone. Usually, most of the crowd is raising their hands. Then I ask if they feel that they were led there by someone else or at least influenced heavily. Led along if you would, even a willing participant but peer pressure or peer acceptance influenced you into this world of substance abuse. I also like to ask if they give Jesus the credit for their freedom from this enslavement, would they stand up. Most of the crowd stands up. Then the question has to be asked of course, did someone influence you to come to Jesus and trust Him for your sobriety?

If you followed someone to your addiction and you followed someone to your freedom, then where are you following someone to today? And the most important question is where are you leading others today.

If you are involved in pornography or any kind of sexual enslavement, the question still remains. Who are you following? Is it your own freedom or do you listen to whoever supports your misguided ideas?

People sit in my office all the time and tell me what they want to do or what they think is right. Usually, it is at a point in their lives where they have floundered very badly. Most often there are other leaders there with them to support and love on them.

I am always emotionally effected by the depth of misery that people find themselves in. Their stories are almost always about them getting deeper and deeper in trouble with the law and their addiction because they cannot surrender their hearts to God and their lives to His authority. They cry out to Him but it is usually with a Santa Claus or magic wand type of expectation, not the "work out your salvation with fear and trembling" kind.

This is when I have to tell them that they must follow someone. So I say "look at the people who love you and have shown their willingness to help you." "Is there anyone who has made it to where you want to go?" "Is there anyone who has the life you want to have?" They usually say "yes." "Where have they gone that you want to go?" They say in some form or other that they want to find God like the person that they admire has found Him. I tell them this "then follow them, listen to them, do what they do, say what they say. Be under their authority as if you were their servant." "They will teach you to know God, to hear Him and feel Him, even to see Him in your life." Then when you know Him you will begin to love the changes and the strength. I promise that if you do this you will have the power to be free."

It is a bold statement but the condition is that you serve and follow. Not every one who starts out on this journey makes it but everyone who continues testifies of the wondrous love that He has for them.

It is a fact that if you want to be a carpenter you should learn from a carpenter. A doctor should learn from a doctor. A disciple should learn from a disciple (like kind begets like kind).

I am a disciple of Jesus Christ, I am sent by my Father and I come in the name of Jesus, follow me and I will show you the way. I am a man who obeys, and others obey me! I am a man in submission and others are submitted to me!! I take orders and others take orders from me!!! Because of this, I know what the outcome is going to be. Jesus says that this was the statement of the greatest faith that He had heard in all of Israel.

It is about this time that the people in my office say "I am going to do what I want to do." They usually say it in different words of course but I help them break it down to this statement.

One day a young man said something to me that really illuminated this very deadly fear of submission to me. He had told me that he was going to leave the drug and alcohol ministry that he was in. So I told him all of the reasons that he should not leave. I reminded him mostly of the misery that he had lived in. He just continued to tell me why he was leaving.

This is when I asked this young man this question. "Have you made a lot of good decisions in your life?" The answer he gave me blew my mind, as he said "why I can't think of even one good decision that I have ever made." Now I was expecting an argument on which decisions were right and wrong but this guy lobbed me a softball and I had to hit it out of the park.

I asked him if he thought that I had made any good decisions in my life?

He said "it is obvious from looking at your life that you have made a lot of good decisions."

I knew that this was going to hurt but I had to say it, "you say that I have made a lot of good decisions and you can tell from looking at my life. By your own admission you can't think of one good decision that you have ever made. So, this is what I hear you saying, you are going to ignore the advice of someone who has made a lot of good decisions to follow the advice of someone who has been 100% wrong on life decisions. Do I have that about right?" He was flabbergasted but had to admit it was right. He then said that he would stay, but alas he left in just a day or so. In the years to follow I have sat with that young man on several occasions to listen to him wail in agony about the situations of his life. I mean wail in agony too, it is not a metaphor. The pain, and dark nights of the soul he has had to endure because of his fear of losing something of himself if he submitted to anyone.

Would we have the courage to say as the Apostles have said to us "follow me as I follow Christ?" To do this we need to understand that the meaning of this is "imitate me as I imitate Christ." We need to take on the full understanding of this and know that we will be used as bait, one way or another as we influence "these little ones" to go deeper with God and know Him. If we don't, then we get used as bait to cause "these little ones to stumble" as Jesus said.

Chapter 23

UNGRATEFUL?
OR COULD NOT SEE!

LUKE RECORDS this story. *"While He was on the way to Jerusalem, He was passing between Samaria and Galilee. As He entered a village, ten leprous men who stood at a distance met Him and they raised their voices, saying, "Jesus, Master, have mercy on us!" When He saw them, He said to them, "Go and show yourselves to the priests." And as they were going, they were cleansed. Now one of them, when he saw that he had been healed, turned back, glorifying God with a loud voice, and he fell on his face at His feet, giving thanks to Him. And he was a Samaritan. Then Jesus answered and said, "Were there not ten cleansed? But the nine--where are they? Was no one found who returned to give glory to God, except this foreigner?" And He said to him, "Stand up and go; your faith has made you well." Now having been questioned by the Pharisees as to when the kingdom of God was coming, He answered them and said, "The kingdom of God is not*

coming with signs to be observed; nor will they say, 'Look, here it is!'
or, 'There it is!' For behold, the kingdom of God is in your midst."

There were ten lepers who were waiting for Jesus and when He came by they called out to Him from a distance, *"Jesus, Master, have mercy on us."* He told them to go show themselves to the priests. As they were going *"they were cleansed,"* it says. One of them turned back to Jesus when he realized that he was healed.

It seems as though all ten were "cleansed" and that it means "healed." One guy turns back because he recognized that he was healed. When Jesus sees him Jesus says, *"were there not ten lepers cleansed?"* *"Where are the nine?"* *"Was no one found to give glory to God except this foreigner?"*

At this point, I am reminded of the many times that I have heard these verses preached on, going all the way back to my early years in the Catholic church. Always then and continuing in the evangelistic churches and Pentecostal churches that I have attended, these verses and this story has always been about the fact that these nine were ungrateful.

Now I know that the ungratefulness of people is legendary and this is definitely about being ungrateful but on a recent morning when I asked the Lord to tell me if this is what He wanted me to get out of these verses, the fact that we are ungrateful, He said "NO" what do you see? I looked and I saw these things.

This man was the only one who did not do what Jesus told him to do.

He realized something greater than the priests was here.

He fell on his face and gave glory to God in front of Jesus and Jesus did not rebuke him.

Jesus told him that *"his faith had made him well."* (Are they not all "well" since they were "all cleansed?") Only this guy is "made well?"

I think the Lord was showing me that the phrase "made you well" is different than cleansed or healed. "Made well" is something that I noticed is not as common as I thought. When I read the teaching of Jesus I get the impression that He is promising abundant life. I don't think that if you get past the confession of faith where they say "I'm fine" that many people are experiencing abundant life. Mostly because they don't expect to experience the "made well" abundance that Jesus said was received by this former leper.

What did this man understand that the others were blind to? Why did he get to be "made well" when they all did what Jesus told them to do? Yet this one man was "made well" when he did not follow the instructions?

Let me recap my thought process here. All ten do the right thing and get in front of the man who is famous for healing. They need healing and according to their law they must stay at a distance or face punishment, even being stoned to death. (People are very serious about not getting leprosy.) These lepers address Him properly, they ask for mercy. He responds and gives them instructions. They go, to do exactly what Jesus says. While they are going they are healed. Then nine of them continue on to the priest, but this one guy turns around and seeks out Jesus. He gets commended and the nine get their gratefulness to God questioned for two thousand years and counting.

Then Jesus says to this one *"your faith has made you well."* Not only has Jesus told him this but He says that by not returning the other nine were not giving glory to God, *"Except this foreigner?"*

What did this guy see that caused him not to obey the instructions? Instructions to do what the law requires them to do as lepers. Was he willing to risk stoning, to go back "glorifying God with a loud voice?" He was not trying to sneak back to Jesus. *"Falling on his face at His feet and giving thanks to Him." "Glorifying God with a loud voice."*

Jesus should have rebuked him and asked why he did not go and show himself to the priests, and why did he fall on his face in front of him? Jesus was only a man after all. Jesus should have said "get up, I am only a man." No, Jesus did not rebuke him for either of these. He said *"go your faith has made you well."*

Although I am thankful for the teachings on this verse about ungratefulness. I am really excited about what it shows as to why this guy turned back, that there is a difference between "healed" and "made well."

I believe that the Samaritan leper saw that something greater than the priests was here. He turned back because the healing of his leprosy helped him to recognize who Jesus was, and praising God while bowing at Jesus feet just makes it more obvious. He saw who Jesus is.

Jesus' own words reveal it. To know who Jesus is and believing that He is God made this Samaritan leper "well" and qualified him to receive all of the rest of what Jesus came to give us. Now this man will "listen to Him" more than he will listen to any other voice. Knowing Jesus' identity has made him well and qualifies him for understanding who Jesus came to make him to be. Sonship of the Father is now possible for him. I bet if we could see back in time we would see that after this man was healed and then made well he joined the crowd that followed along wherever Jesus went. I would bet that he understood that to receive eternal life he would have to answer the call of Jesus to "follow Me" and he did just that.

Chapter 24

WHO IS THIS MAN WHO CALLS HIMSELF THE SON?

NOW HAVING *been questioned by the Pharisees as to when the kingdom of God was coming, He answered them and said, "The kingdom of God is not coming with signs to be observed; nor will they say, 'Look, here it is!' or, 'There it is!' For behold, the kingdom of God is in your midst."*

Jesus was the King of Heaven and Lord over all the earth. That made Him the Kingdom of God in person and all lepers "cleansed, healed and made well" should be falling on their face to worship. Whenever I see leaders that ignore the worship of Him it makes me wonder what they have seen in their lives. Are they like the nine who just experience the miracle and go on to religion or do they actually see that something is different about Jesus? The action of ignoring His presence raises the question of whether they have seen the Kingdom of God in Jesus or are they just impressed with Him.

Seeing that there is something different about Him and seeing the Father in Him is a most life changing revelation. Not all see it. Not all look for it. Jesus thought that it was important so He said in answer to the request to "show us the Father," "*if you have seen me you have seen the Father.*" Not everyone sees this in Jesus so they try to go around Him to a direct relationship to the Father. I don't understand this. Some people try to relate to God as David did or Solomon, even Moses, Elijah, Joshua or Abraham. Jesus said it as plain as day that "*no one comes to the Father except through me,*" also Jesus said that "*I and the Father are one,*" and again "*if you have seen Me you have seen the Father.*" Here in this story Jesus did not rebuke this healed leper who worshiped Him. It could not be plainer to see what Jesus and the Father expect us to do to be "made well;" being "made well" includes understanding that Jesus is in the Father and the Father is in Jesus.

Do they see that when they pray "let your kingdom come" they are inviting Jesus into their lives, because they are inviting the Father's kingdom?

Sometimes I wonder, if people see Jesus the way that they see antibiotics. Take a little Jesus and you have killed the sin in your life, then you can get to know and obey God. Follow a religion like a prescription and all problems should clear up in a few days. See disease and you just take a little Jesus to it, wave His name over the problem and whammo, done!!! No, I don't have a king, no, I don't have any rules, but I do know a name.

Grateful? This ex-leper was falling on his face praising in a loud voice, bringing attention to himself, he was not cleared by the priest to be in public yet he did not care. This leper knew that he had found the Key holder to unlock the doors of all his hopes and dreams that had been way out of his reach as a leper. If he had a wife he could hug her, if he had children he could play with them. Simple dreams maybe, but the whole world was now possible to him and he knew who this was who gave it to him. He knew what he had been given and he was not ashamed and he was willing to risk all to deliver the message. This Jesus is the Almighty and He has come to us, I will praise Him, I will make myself a spectacle to proclaim who He is.

At the time Jesus called the Apostles they were something other than the men who the Bible is written about. His example and teaching as found in the gospels is extreme and shocking. My life being spent studying these teachings has caused a great many difficult decisions in my life and not one do I regret.

I see the examples in the Old Testament that Jesus did not follow, like the Sabbath requirements, He says that something greater than the Sabbath is here. Something greater than the temple is here.

Today people want to make it more complicated than Jesus and the Father made it. Jesus said to His disciples *"follow Me"* and the Father said on the mount of transfiguration in the presence of Moses and Elijah *"this is my son listen to Him."* How simple is this?

Jesus said, *"if you say to this mountain move, it will move." "If you lay hands on the sick they will recover." "Ask whatsoever you will in my name and it will be done."*

What I say can move a mountain, which means that words have power to change the location that God put it in. My touch will heal the sick, also powerful! My will would get its way every time since "whatsoever you will" is the condition of that promise. Jesus said to the leper, *"your faith has made you well,"* Jesus was not taking credit for making the man well. He said, "your faith made you well."

My words!

My will!

My faith!

What does it mean? What does it take?

Let's try to "listen to Him."

In the next story about the two prayers, Jesus asks, *"When the son of man returns will He find any faith left on the earth?"* In the story after this, about the rich young ruler, He asks that young man *"why do you call Me good, only God is good."* I believe that the secret here is not the name that we believe in or the way in which we try to strengthen our faith. It is first, and foremost the understanding of who it is that we have faith in. A Jesus by any other identity is not as sweet. Or put in another way, we need to answer two questions. Who is Jesus? And who does that make me?

The identity of Jesus and our identity seems to be the message that Jesus keeps giving. The evidences that we need to establish to determine whether we have answered these questions correctly is very simple.

We need to ask ourselves more questions. First, do we love our brother as we have been loved? Jesus said, "*by this all men will know that you are my disciples.*" This standard is clear, all men and as we have been loved. Not the usual Christian answer of loving as we have loved ourselves but as we have been loved. The evidence of discipleship.

The second question is, who do we believe that Jesus is? As the leper realized, do we know that Jesus is greater than the law and the prophets? Is He greater than Moses and Elijah, as the apostles learned on the mountain. Who do we believe in? Do we call Him good? Only God is good, is that what you are saying? It seems that the identity of Jesus was His most important teaching to the Jews. He kept asking them and rewarding them when they believed correctly no matter who they were. Samaritan foreigners or Roman Centurions, Jesus was impressed with those who recognized His identity. It seems to be the number one requirement and purpose of a Jesus disciple, that we answer the question, who is Jesus?

Which brings us to the next question. Who does that make you? With the disciples in a boat in a storm, they did not try to calm the storm since they did not believe that they could do it, or with the boy and his father, "*I asked your disciples and they could not do it.*" Jesus was not happy that they were not getting it. He said, "*You unbelieving and perverted generation, how long shall I be with you? How long shall I put up with you? Bring him here to Me.*" Or with the five thousand when the disciples said to Jesus "*This place is desolate and the hour is already late; so send the crowds away, that they may go into the villages and buy food for themselves."*

Jesus answered, *"They do not need to go away; you give them something to eat!"* I think it is clear, Jesus wanted them to become something other than what they were. He wanted them to be "born again" into "new creatures" who thought different and talked different. Men who believed that who they were and who they believed in could make them storm calmers, demon chasers, healers and Kingdom preachers not to mention becoming men who could meet the needs of thousands on a single day.

Peter eventually got it and he jerked a crippled man to his feet while saying, *"silver and gold I do not have, but what I do have I give to you, in the name of Jesus Christ get up and walk."* I think the story is awesome but the words "what I do have I give" are not often modeled in our times, mostly because we don't know who we are in Jesus. Peter is one of the guys we all agree that we are supposed to imitate. Yet it is rare that I hear this imitated. I have been trying and I have begun to have incredible results. Now I haven't pushed any blind men out in front of traffic to see if they could dodge it as they see. This is the kind of risk that Peter took, if that lame man had not been healed he would have come crashing down in a heap. Peter would probably been stoned and Christianity maybe hindered from spreading.

I think some of the right questions are: Do we have the evidence of discipleship in our lives? Do we love as we have been loved? Do we believe in the right Jesus? Who do we say that He is? Is he good? Is He God? Who do we think that He wants us to become? He said that we would do these things that we see Him do, and greater things than these will we do.

When the Pharisees questioned Him about the Kingdom of God, Jesus answered, He said, *"The kingdom of God is not coming with signs to be observed; nor will they say, 'Look, here it is!' or, 'There it is!' For behold, the kingdom of God is in your midst."* Jesus is the Kingdom of God! And He has given us the job of being the Kingdom of God with Him. Signs and wonders do not determine if the

Kingdom is here, we do! Where we are is supposed to be where the Kingdom is. Signs and wonders follow us!

Like salt we will flavor and preserve. Drawing men to the Lord's mercy and power. Like living water, we will satisfy and quench men's thirst for God. He will make His home in us.

Healings, signs and wonders will follow us. It is evident since these men that Jesus was teaching demonstrated all of these things. He taught them many things and the study of the things He taught must be our most important search. As I "follow Him" and "Listen to Him," I will become like Him and the "greater things than these will you do," will become evident in my life and to the people around me who, "follow me as I follow Christ."

Jesus is the Father, if you have seen Jesus you have seen the Father. He is God Almighty, and He makes His home in me. Jesus is Mercy and Grace, He is the very definition of these gifts. He is the King of Heaven and Lord over all of the earth. Where He is, is the Kingdom of God.

He lives in me and as I submit to His teaching and consent to being born again, I will be His disciple and where I go will be where the Kingdom of God goes. Those who see me will see Him.

There is even more promised, more given to those who answer the call!!!!

Chapter 25

FOLLOWERS HAVE
THE LIGHT

"THEN JESUS *again spoke to them, saying, "I am the Light of the world; he who follows Me will not walk in the darkness, but will have the Light of life."*

One night I got up to go to the restroom in my own home. I was half asleep and could not figure out where I was. There was no moon and we had no night light on in the house at all. It was as dark as a blackout. I reached out and realized that I was reaching from memory. There were certain expectations in my mind that I would find the wall here, the light switch would be right over there. It was not where it was supposed to be. As you probably have guessed, these things were where they were supposed to be, I was not.

As if coming out of a fog I began to realize that I was still looking for the restroom on the cruise ship that I had spent the last ten days on. I had gone to that restroom at least twenty times in the middle of the night and it had become a habit already. On the first night home, because it was a moonless night, I was still stumbling in my slumber to the wrong restroom. As you might also guess, I was bouncing off of walls stubbing my toe in the dark.

I had not moved the restroom. I had not moved anything, the bedroom was just as I had left it and I have lived in this home for a long time. The darkness and the condition that I was in, coming out of a deep sleep had deceived me. If there had just been a little bit of light I would probably not have even remembered getting up that night at all. But here I was standing in the hallway to the living room feeling around for the sink that should have been right in front of me. I had made the right turns and taken the right number of steps. I should be opening the door and stepping up to enter the cruise ship restroom.

But the floor feels wrong and the toilet is not in front of me! As my confusion fades I realize what I have done. I begin to understand that I am lost in the darkness and I am nowhere near where I thought that I was. As I began to realize where I was, I thought about the light switch that should be right about there!! It was not, but the wall was. I felt down the wall until a door frame jammed my finger. It hurt bad! Then my toe slammed into a chair leg, I can not describe the pain, I don't remember ever having such acute pain in my life. All that I could think of was how good it was going to feel when the pain went away. The good news was that the chair leg revealed where I was and now I really knew which way the wall was. I found it, then the light switch. The light nearly blinded me, I was unable to move but only for a moment.

You know it is amazing how much easier it is to navigate your own house and make your way painlessly around it, even getting where you need to get, relieving pressure that you need to relieve, with a little bit of light.

As I was getting back into bed I had some time to reflect on this experience and wonder how a man can get so lost in his own world. The mind is a incredible organ. I was lost and hurting myself in the place where I am the most comfortable. Just because of darkness!! Or the lack of light!!!

However you choose to look at it.

Just when I thought that I knew exactly where I was, (the lost and confused world think that they know where they are too) I realized that I was lost. So many of my friends have told me similar stories, stories about their lives. Like when they were in the darkness and when the big steel doors slammed shut on the jail cell that they had been put in. My friends say it was as if a light went on. It is strange the way they explain it. The light went on and they then realized that they were in the dark and needed the Light of the World. They got saved because they now figured out that they needed help.

Jesus says here in this verse that He is the Light of the World and if you "follow Him" you would not walk in the darkness, but have the Light. If someone had just come along with a little light when I was stumbling in the dark I probably would not have jammed my finger or stubbed my toe. If someone walked in the world shining the Light of the World into the darkness, then how many people would avoid the trapping of this world's systems?

Let me give you an exercise to try at home. Turn off the light in a room that you can make dark. Let your eyes be filled with the darkness, then turn on the switch and see how fast everything becomes clear. Also, do it several times noticing different things about the darkness and the light. One of my favorite things to see is that the darkness does not fight back or ever win. Also the darkness never loses when the light is turned off. I wonder then, if you can ever afford to turn off the Light in your life. You know, just for a night to party. Do you ever not lose?

If only those who go by the name Christian would study Jesus and His teachings as the Father instructed us to, if they would take to heart that the only way to the Father is through Jesus. Not ignoring that when once they have had a revelation of the teachings of Jesus and have begun to get a vision of Him and what He actually says, to not always mix it with what everybody else says. If they would do these things, then they would see Jesus and only then will they have seen the Father.

If you want to know what the Father wants, then see what Jesus wants. Maybe you want to hear the Father? Then hear Jesus! This is how the Bible says that you will see signs and wonders. Build your faith by hearing of the Word of God! And the Word became flesh and dwelt among us, hear about Jesus. Want faith, signs and wonders? See Jesus and "listen to Him." "Follow Him" and you will have THE LIGHT. More importantly, you will not walk in darkness and stub your toe or worse. Maybe you won't ever be lost. Maybe you won't ever be bait to lure someone away to the darkness ever again. If you have THE LIGHT, then maybe you can lead them out of the darkness where they are stubbing their toes and worse. First your loved ones and then the "one another's" that Jesus told us to love. I am sure that if THE LIGHT shined bright into the world, many who are lost in the darkness would come to THE LIGHT.

Some even rejected Jesus and I know that I am at best a reflection, yet I am on my way to understanding what it means to answer the call to "follow me" that Jesus refers to here in this verse. He means that we should imitate Him. Actually be Him, not be David or Elijah but Him. To "follow Him" means that I must be like Him and then the promise that He made would be a promise made to me. That I "would not walk in darkness," but have THE LIGHT. Amen, I want it, I should say I want Him, which means I will follow you Jesus. I will shine THE LIGHT into the darkness and lead many out of the darkness and into THE LIGHT.

This means that I will be THE LIGHT as well. I will become responsible for who gets to see THE LIGHT and comes to see the Father, to know the Father, to hear the Father. Who gets baptized in His love is up to me and the only condition is will I answer the call to "follow Me" that Jesus has placed before all of us.

I will not be bait and risk the millstone and sea. I will not walk in darkness and stumble and stub my toe. I will not be lost!!

Even in my own home I have installed light switches with locator lights in them. They are easy to see in the dark, even these little lights have power to lead me to the right place. I'm ready for the power outages as well with battery backed up night lights in the halls and bathrooms. Light is important if you don't want to be swallowed up in darkness. Jesus said "I am the Light of the world; he who follows Me will not walk in the darkness, but will have THE LIGHT of life." I will follow you Jesus, my house is ready, my life is ready, I am teaching my church to be ready with the admonition to follow me as I follow Christ and I won't lead them astray. I see the darkness flee from people's lives as THE LIGHT comes on and they are chasing the darkness away!!!

Chapter 26

MY SHEEP HEAR MY VOICE

"IT WAS *winter, and Jesus was walking in the temple in the portico of Solomon. The Jews then gathered around Him, and were saying to Him, "How long will You keep us in suspense? If You are the Christ, tell us plainly."*

"Jesus answered them, "I told you, and you do not believe; the works that I do in My Father's name, these testify of Me. But you do not believe because you are not of My sheep. My sheep hear My voice, and I know them, and they follow Me; and I give eternal life to them, and they will never perish; and no one will snatch them out of My hand. My Father, who has given them to Me, is greater than all; and no one is able to snatch them out of the Father's hand. I and the Father are one."

When we see lightning and rain we say it is storming outside. We don't have to get wet, shocked or cold to know this, the signs are the symptoms. There are a million of these examples and other metaphors to use to describe what Jesus is saying. Jesus says that *the works that I do in My Father's name, these testify of Me.* He does not have to say "I am the Christ" they should be able to determine this from the works that He does in His Father's name. Jesus is saying the works tell the story more than Him saying it. In their day many said "I am the Christ." Jesus did not say this but He is saying that it should be evident, like looking out the window and seeing the storm. There are several things here that are interesting.

First, He says *"you do not believe because you are not of My sheep."* Some believe that this supports the idea that a person has to be one of the sheep before they believe. What it really means is they have not come seeking God so they don't believe. They see the same evidence that the sheep see but they don't believe. Not believing causes them to not be counted among the sheep. They see the works and Jesus says that by these works I have told them. Seeing this same evidence (the works) they can't figure out who is doing it or who Jesus is.

Another great thing that I see from these verses is that His sheep hear His voice. The men of His time were surrounded by sheep. There were flocks in the fields around their country and the profession of shepherd was common. The shepherds would gather their sheep together in a sheep pen when they were gathered in a town or when they grazed their sheep together in the same field. When the shepherd was ready to leave, he simply raised his voice in a call that was known to his sheep and his sheep would follow him. This is how they would separate their sheep from the others. It was the sheep who knew who they belonged to and knew their master's voice, when they heard his voice they followed him. The following of his voice is what made them his sheep and him their master.

Which brings us back to Jesus and this most incredible statement. He says that you are not His sheep if you don't follow Him. You won't follow Him if you don't recognize His voice.

Most importantly to me is that He is saying that His works are His voice. I know in my life those works certainly are the works of healing, deliverance and salvation. But the most enjoyable in the life of following are the fruit of the Spirit, "*love, joy, peace, patience, kindness, goodness, faithfulness, gentleness, and self-control.*" I would follow Him for these alone and yet the works that He does, He does in the name of the Father, His Father, that He causes to be my Father.

I have decided to follow Him and be His sheep and recognize His works in my life as His shepherd's call. I will answer the Shepherd's call to come follow and imitate Him. This is the only evidence that I am His sheep in this story. It is that I hear Him and follow. The evidence of these truths, to the rest of the world is seen when I imitate His love for me. He says they will know who I follow by this love.

He also says that He did these miraculous works in His Father's name. I have never read anywhere that Jesus ever said "God please take the storm away and I pray in My Father's name." It never happened once and yet He says here that He did every work in His Father's name. He healed every disease and infirmity, cast out many demons, calmed storms and cursed fig trees, yet not once do I remember Him using the form of prayer that we use today, "I ask in Jesus name." He simply did the miraculous and because these things that He commanded, happened, they should have believed that He came from the Father and that He was the Christ because of the works that He did. If you don't believe them, then you won't believe Me if I tell you in words.

Jesus commanded miracles to show the people that the Father loved them and did not want them to suffer the results of sin in the world. This is the definition of "in My Father's name." Power demonstrated to set the prisoner free from sin, sickness, and disease because God loves us so much, is done in the name of the Father. The most loving and miraculous of these is the forgiveness of sins. It took the most work and caused the most suffering, requiring a "Lamb of God who takes away the sins of the world." This is the love of the Father that He sent Jesus to die on the cross for our sins. This is the very definition of "in the name of the Father" and "in the name of Jesus." The works that I do in my Father's name, these testify of Jesus.

The works we do, they testify of us, they tell the story of whose sheep we are. They are His voice to the world and those who know His voice will hear Him and "follow Him." People who do this, know who He is and learn who they are in Him. They will come in His name, pray in His name, do in His name and not just try to use a name that does not describe who they are.

Chapter 27

LAKELAND

RECENTLY IN America we had a revival and people were getting very excited, a friend of mine turned on his computer to show me this great thing. I watched for ten seconds and could not keep the words from coming out of my mouth, I said, "Oh no." Rebellion was the fruit I saw and this evangelist was bragging about being rejected by the church, not mourning it. Since ten seconds was not enough of an inspection of the fruit, I decided to go and see for myself.

I took seven of my Interns and staff with me and went to the revival. I listened intently and wanted nothing more than to see this healing outpouring. I had waited all my life for what this was being called.

I listened to seven messages, some on the computer, some in person at the venues, and I never heard one substantive thing. Nothing was said that I could believe in or change from. The miracles were called miracles whether there was visible evidence or not. People got up from their wheel chair then rode that same chair out of the place. This is all that I saw, not one visible healing that could be substantiated. People I know who went at other times told me that they saw substantial miracles but I did not.

What was very visible was hype, rebellion and a pride that he did not adhere to conventional methods of church. All he did was model a very common method of conducting healing services. I had been to many just like it in my younger years, there was nothing special about this. Even the offerings were exactly the same. Fifty people are supposed to give $250.00 and if you do, you will receive a 100 fold return. Playing on people's faith and manipulating them.

Since this revival has folded, I have heard reports of excessive drinking and inappropriate relationships and even divorce from his wife, and this may surprise you, but I don't blame him.

He was doing what he was taught was alright. It is the rest of us that refuse to examine the fruit, that don't hold leaders accountable to fruit bearing that are at fault.

Some may ask where is the harm in what happened here, because many people were touched and even healed. This very thought caused me concern when I was there. So I asked the Lord what I should see here and He said ,"look."

What I saw was many people loving the Lord and basking in His presence with great joy and expectation. He was inhabiting the worship and love of His people and where His people were there He was. It was beautiful.

So what is the problem, you may ask? Well, what I also saw was fathers and mothers taking their children up to the stage in an attempt to rescue them from afflictions like Down's Syndrome, Cerebral Palsy, in addition to other people of various illnesses. They were not allowed on stage to be prayed for, and may have come away with the feeling of having been rejected by God.

The first casualty in a hyped revival is faith, faith that moves mountains. Do people who are hurting go home from a hyped revival with more faith in the fact that God loves them or less? Will those parents believe for their child's healing any longer? Will they go again when they feel rejected by God? God did not reject them, the screeners did because their disease or affliction was too visible.

Will they miss the next real healing outpouring or not, because they did not want to hear any more hype? Would they allow themselves to believe and risk the great pain that having your hope dashed causes. I am the Father of a son with Down's Syndrome and I can feel their pain.

Will they trust that God would heal their loved ones anywhere or anytime without the hype?

When these same leaders give their endorsement for the next revival I know that even if I love them I will not trust their judgement as easily as before. It was the leaders who endorsed this revival that convinced many (even over their own uneasy feelings) to go all the way to Florida. I know that I will not follow so easily.

I recently had a healing conference at my church. There were really good testimonies of healing. There was teaching that really caused our faith to grow. But I noticed something about the people who went with me to Florida, they did not want to be at these meetings and they did not go forward for prayer for healing. As I talked with them, I realized they were mad at God and the evangelist in Florida, they were disillusioned. They were hesitant to let themselves get high expectations again. Now this by itself is a true following crisis.

This group that had gone to Florida was not intimidated by failure, they had been trying to walk on water in my swimming pool and when they sank they just climbed out and tried again. It was not that it must be done according to their expectations. It was that they had trusted the leaders who had endorsed this evangelist to them and they had followed these leader's advice. I think my interns felt betrayed when they found out that worldwide leaders knew the evangelist was rebellious to leadership, and the fact that these leaders reportedly knew there was "excessive drinking," and "inappropriate relationships with women," yet they endorsed this as a sovereign move of God. As if somehow you can have a revival with the God of Holiness and behave in a blatantly rebellious manner.

There has been a trend in recent years at least in the circles of Christians who are God chasing (I mean people who value the presence of God), to value anointing over character. I think this is what happened in Florida. We forgot to look at the character in a man and only listened to his words. You will never do well in any venture connected with God's presence when you forget that "no good fruit comes from a bad tree," I don't mean this man but I do mean rebellion and selfishness.

I will tell you that the leaders who laid hands on this evangelist and endorsed him have my greatest respect and loyalty.

I have examined the fruit of these men and the others and it is good. I will follow their lead and go where they say it is good to go. All I ask of them is that they value and respect the follower as much as the followers respect them. Protect us from the events that will damage faith and lead us to events that will build our faith.

The thing that I do know about revival is that there is no reason to hype it. Jesus never did, the Apostles never did, it wasn't hyped in Toronto and it was not hyped in the 1970's with the salvation revival of the Jesus movement. No, it was like a migration to Jesus by all the hungry people.

Now I don't want to be included in all the people who hate and write letters to all the leaders who supported this revival. I just want to make the point that you do not get good fruit from a bad tree (I am not referring to this evangelist but the behavior that was called anointing) and the instructions of Jesus were to bear fruit in all seasons. Even "dig around the roots a little and give it fertilizer and water." Give the fruit a chance, make sure the fruit is good, and definitely inspect it.

If you believe that you are a leader, then try to inspect the fruit before you endorse anyone claiming great revival. The fruit of someone is not difficult to see or hear. No good thing can come from rebellion.

The worst thing that happened from this revival was that this evangelist is darn near destroyed by his promotion and he is a person who is wholly loved by God. He is a person who I happen to know has a great heart as many of my friends would testify. He just should not have been promoted to this level of world wide exposure to our enemies.

Our people deserve our expertise in fruit acknowledgement to be for their benefit.

There will be testimonies for years of God's touch in people's lives from them going to this venue because we have a very loving Father. His presence always inhabits the praises of His people. He is "the rewarder of those who diligently seek Him."

When God shows up in a crowd of people it is not bad fruit that He blesses. It is the fulfillment of his promise to love and inhabit the adoration of His people and make His home with them.

Chapter 28

THE RICH
YOUNG RULER

"A RULER *questioned Him, saying, "Good Teacher, what shall I do
to inherit eternal life?" And Jesus said to him, "Why do you call Me
good? No one is good except God alone. You know the commandments, 'DO NOT COMMIT ADULTERY, DO NOT MURDER,
DO NOT STEAL, DO NOT BEAR FALSE WITNESS, HONOR
YOUR FATHER AND MOTHER'." And he said, "All these things
I have kept from my youth." When Jesus heard this, He said to him,
"One thing you still lack; sell all that you possess and distribute it
to the poor, and you shall have treasure in heaven; and come follow
Me." But when he had heard these things, he became very sad, for
he was extremely rich. And Jesus looked at him and said, "How hard
it is for those who are wealthy to enter the kingdom of God! For it
is easier for a camel to go through the eye of a needle than for a rich
man to enter the kingdom of God." They who heard it said, "Then*

who can be saved?" But He said, "The things that are impossible with people are possible with God."

Jesus is asked a question here about the inheriting of eternal life. He answers the question with a question about the name by which he was addressed. *"Why do you call Me good,"* Jesus says *"No one is good except God alone."* It seems that what He is asking this young man is the question, who do you say that I am, are you calling me God? The identity of Jesus again seems to be the most important subject in answer to the question, "what shall I do to inherit eternal life?" All of my life as a teacher I have believed that the statement "sell all that you possess and distribute it to the poor" was the important "one thing you still lack." I saw that Jesus actually said to him "one thing you still lack" then He told him two things. The instructions to "sell all that you possess" was the answer to the statement "All these things I have kept from my youth." This guy had not kept the commandments and Jesus was telling him that to keep the commandments you had to love your poor neighbor as you loved yourself. No doubt this rich man had bought many comforts for himself and not bought those same comforts for his neighbor. So he still lacked one thing to fulfill the obedience of the commandments. Go do this and "sell all that you possess and distribute it to the poor, and you shall have treasure in heaven" and do one more thing, "come follow Me." This seems to be the answer to the question about eternal life, just: "come and follow me."

The purpose that his coming and following would accomplish would be this young man's understanding the identity of Jesus so that he could answer the question, "who do you say that I am," which is implied in this conversation with the question, "why do you call me good?" Are you saying I am God, because "only God is good."

Jesus said to the rich young ruler that he must sell all that he has and give it to the poor to fulfill the law but if he wants eternal life he must "come and follow Me." The reason for following Him is so he can find out who Jesus is and gain the eternal life that he is trying to obtain.

The men who were already following were under constant pressure from Jesus that they should become storm calmers, crowd feeders, demon commanders, in addition to disease healers, all while they preach the kingdom. Jesus even tells them when He sends them out, *"Whatever city you enter and they receive you, eat what is set before you and heal those in it who are sick, and say to them, The kingdom of God has come near to you. But whatever city you enter and they do not receive you, go out into its streets and say, even the dust of your city which clings to our feet we wipe off in protest against you; yet be sure of this, that the kingdom of God has come near."* They were expected to follow and imitate Jesus until they became the Kingdom of God that is near.

The answer to the question "what shall I do to inherit eternal life" that Jesus gave was "Why do you call Me good? No one is good except God alone." Only God is good, He wants to know, are you saying that I am God? Do you believe in the fact that I am the Christ? In any search for answers we must first ask this, who is Jesus to you? First this must be answered! If the answer is not that He is good, as God is good, then we should look elsewhere for the eternal life. If the answer is that He is the Christ the son of the living God, then we are on the right track, Jesus has the answers.

What you still lack after answering this question is that you still need to "follow Him." If following Him is defined as imitating or becoming like Him, then the next most important question to answer is, what is your identity? Who you are is what Jesus wants you to understand from "following Him." Who are you going to become from "following Him?" Are you going to become a storm calmer and demon commander like Jesus ? Are you going to become the Kingdom of God carrier in your person that He was?

The cities that He sends you to need to "receive you" and when you heal the sick you are supposed to tell them that "The kingdom of God has come near to you." Jesus did not go to these cities, His followers went to these cities, followers who had answered the question "who do you say that I am" and were in the process of understanding who that caused them to become.

History tells us that these disciples became men who carried the Kingdom of God with them and command the power that is in the Kingdom of God!

The rich young ruler was given the opportunity to shed his earthly responsibilities and drop his net and answer Jesus' call to "follow Me" but it says; *"he became very sad, for he was extremely rich."* He traded who he could become for what he already had. Jesus then discusses how hard it is to leave all to "follow him" if you are rich. "A bird in hand (wealth and comfort and security) is better than two in the bush" might have been his thinking.

The dilemma is would you trade all that you have to be the carrier of the Kingdom of God and inherit eternal life? Would you trade all to have it be true that where you went the Kingdom of God went? This man found a line he would not cross. The people at this gathering understood this, we know by the question they asked next. "Then who can be saved?"

The identity of Jesus is the question, who do you say that He is? The answer is, He is the "Christ the Son of the living God." If this is your answer then what is your identity? Does the "kingdom of God" come near to those who come near to you?

Will you pay any price, do any deeds, slay dragons if you have to, to become the person that God has called you to be? Unlike the rich young ruler, will you do as much to inherit Eternal Life?

In following Jesus you will hear Him say, *"You of little faith! Do not worry then, saying, What will we eat? or What will we drink? or What will we wear for clothing? But seek first His kingdom and His righteousness, and all these things will be added to you. And again, so do not worry about tomorrow; for tomorrow will care for itself. Each day has enough trouble of its own."* Like this young man in our story will you consider your savings and annuities, your wealth and securities as too much to give up for "following Jesus?"

What line won't you cross? What price won't you pay? What distance won't you travel? Who would you love more than God? If there are crosses in your future will your prayers be, "not my will but thine

O Lord?" And will you pick up your cross and "follow Him" even to Eternal Life?

We will continue to look at this story and see if we can find the treasures that Jesus has placed before us, finding out what it means to have Eternal Life and to answer Jesus' call to "follow Me."

Chapter 29

SACRED COWS

A SACRED cow is a cow found in a country where cows are considered divine, these cows live next to many children who are dying of starvation. No one will eat these cows even when death by starvation of these children is so awful to behold. If someone did feed the cow or even the milk to these children, they could be punished severely.

The rich young ruler from our story had asked a very important question that every person alive should ask, "What must I do to inherit eternal life?" This question led to the answer being something that he would not do.

The revelation the people had was that this man could not be saved, so they asked this question. "Then who can be saved?" Which led Jesus to answer, "*The things that are impossible with people are possible with God.*" This did not warm the cockles of their hearts (they did not accept this answer). Peter said, "*Behold, we have left our own homes and followed You.*" And Jesus said to them, "*Truly I say to you, there is no one who has left house or wife or brothers or parents or children, for the sake of the kingdom of God, who will not receive many times as much at this time and in the age to come, eternal life."*

This young ruler had found a line that he would not cross to obtain eternal life. He even called Jesus "good teacher" to which Jesus asked Him if he really meant this. He seemed to know who Jesus was. Then Jesus told him if he wanted to have eternal life he had to "come and follow me" (cross that line) and "sell all that you possess and distribute it to the poor" (eat that cow). Either way the rich young ruler could not do what he perceived Jesus was telling him to do. He had found a line he would not cross. He had met his sacred cow. He would starve his children and let the cow live, for in it he thought he would be secure and avoid consequences.

This causes me to consider for my life and ask my congregation if in their lives, "what is your sacred cow? What is it you won't do or give up to obtain eternal life?"

If you are thinking that I am advocating salvation by works I am not. I am trying to "listen to Jesus." He asked this man to do something and he could not do it. I have asked my people what they would not do. Jesus said there was a list of things that would qualify as actions that would make it impossible to be His disciple. He said if they would not do these things then "you cannot be my disciple." If this is the case and this young man could not do what he was told to do then maybe there are things that we won't do to inherit eternal life. Ask yourself as I have, what those things might be? What wouldn't I give?

I have asked my church to consider these things and ask the Father to reveal them to us. Things like, do I have anyone that I will not forgive? As we know Jesus said plainly that "if you do not forgive you will not be forgiven." Try to inherit eternal life without being forgiven! To forfeit eternal life to hold onto unforgiveness would be tragic since forgiveness is the "free gift of God." Free, yet forfeitable! What won't you do? I do know some people who have given up the addictions of their past yet refuse to give up the life and identity of their past. The way of living they were addicted to as well as the substance. I have known those who just like the rich young ruler refuse to walk away from the life they had. I know many more people who refuse to walk away from the teachings of the Proverbs to save for tomorrow in spite of Jesus teaching that to save for tomorrow is to not trust in God but to trust in yourself. Here you have two conflicting teachings both from the word of God and it brings you to the same place as the rich young ruler found himself. What is it you won't do? What is your sacred cow?

In the story of the sheep and goats Jesus said *"Truly I say to you, to the extent that you did not do it to one of the least of these, you did not do it to Me. These will go away into eternal punishment, but the righteous into eternal life."* "Eternal life? Eternal punishment?" Have you read the descriptions of these? Did He really mean "eternal punishment?" "Weeping and gnashing of teeth" ?"Outer darkness?" Is this worth whatever it is that qualifies as "cannot be my disciple" or does not "follow me?" Does saving up for tomorrow and listening to Solomon instead of Jesus really qualify as being worth losing eternal life? When "without faith it is impossible to please God."

I wonder what could possibly be worth that? Let us continue to examine this story.

Chapter 30

FOR THE SAKE OF THE KINGDOM

"THEY WHO *heard it said, "Then who can be saved?" But He said, "The things that are impossible with people are possible with God." Peter said, "Behold, we have left our own homes and followed You."*

In answer to Peter's statement about leaving homes, Jesus continues *"and He said to them, "Truly I say to you, there is no one who has left house or wife or brothers or parents or children, for the sake of the kingdom of God, who will not receive many times as much at this time and in the age to come, eternal life."*

This means that even if I do cross the line and answer Jesus' call to "come, follow Me," if that means trusting Him for my finances and my tomorrows, that I may lose everything. In Peter's question he states, I do lose my home, I risk losing my life, but I gain "many times more" ? Eternal life is the promise right? Yes, but "at this time" I will "receive many times more" than what I left behind. When counting cost, I don't think we would call a "many times more" return, a loss. To give a real picture of what Jesus is telling us, He is saying to receive much we must lose much. Matthew records this thought so clearly when he quotes Jesus saying, "*For whoever wishes to save his life will lose it; but whoever loses his life for My sake will find it. For what will it profit a man if he gains the whole world and forfeits his soul? Or what will a man give in exchange for his soul? For the Son of Man is going to come in the glory of His Father with His angels, and WILL THEN REPAY EVERY MAN ACCORDING TO HIS DEEDS.*" WOW!!!

The rich young ruler walked away from the "many times more" and the "eternal life" for what he had in his hand, which was obviously not fulfilling him since he did not have the promise of eternal life.

This would be defined as the sacred cow that we spoke about. I have known many people with sacred cows. Most because of the evil that other people have put on them through neglect and abuse. Some through wrong teachings but the majority came through the selfishness of others, which then was inherited as their own selfishness, and so on.

These sacred cows cause us to have fears and trust issues that we don't think that we can handle. I once told the Lord that I did not think that if one of my babies were to die that I would be able to serve Him any longer. I think that this clearly is the line. I want "eternal life" and I want the "many times more" in this life but I promise you that a statement like that to God only puts my eternity in question. Not because God is going to stomp the yard on me but because it puts my children on the throne of my life and nothing does very well there except the Lord.

I knew a lady in Spokane, Washington who was a young girl when she gave her heart to the Lord. Her name was Doris and she loved roller skating. She was told and convinced that she had to give up roller skating if she wanted eternal life. She chose eternal life. I don't believe that we have to choose between Jesus' command and roller skating to have eternal life, but the saints who were teaching her believed this and they convinced her. This understanding brought her to the decision to choose which she loved more and she chose wisely. She would do this to "follow Jesus."

I know many people who believe tithing is a New Testament command. I believe it is taught as the standard of giving in many Christian circles. "*Will man rob God?*" is quoted in these pleas to get people to tithe. Yet, nowhere in the new covenant is tithing taught. When Peter had his chance to say what is required of gentile Christians he did not mention tithing. Even in the old covenant tithing is never about money. It is about increase, it is an easy leap to bring the word increase to mean money since today we seldom trade in any thing else. The result is, at least in the west, the church has been reported to have only two to five percent of its attendees tithing, even when the leaders of most Christian movements teach it as "robbing God" if you don't tithe. Several people come to my mind who believe strongly that tithing is the only standard of obedience, yet when asked if they do it they say "I can't." What would happen to these poor young rulers of their own lives if they had to come face to face with the answer that Jesus gave, "sell all that you possess and distribute it to the poor," not ten percent, "all." If ten percent of our income or roller skating is more than we could do then what do we do with the list of Luke 14 when he said that if you don't "pick up your cross and follow Me; you cannot be my disciple." Sounds like a heck of a lot more than just ten percent or roller skating.

The life that has anything on its throne except God is a life that is in danger of dysfunction and the thing that is put above God is uncovered from being under the shadow of His wing. It is unprotected.

"*There is no one who has left house or wife or brothers or parents or children, for the sake of the kingdom of God, will not receive many times as much*" Does that mean that anyone who does not do these things will fail to receive? And what does this, "for the sake of the kingdom," mean anyway? Could it mean that if you give to receive, save up to secure your future, trust in yourselves (your mighty right hand), or you trust in and refuse to live without your savings accounts and life insurance that you are not doing it,"for the sake of the kingdom?" What Peter said was,"behold, we have left our own homes and followed You." So to give up all, including putting children and home and even life, behind their devotion to following Jesus was to do it "for the sake of the kingdom," reaping the rewards of the "many times as much" that Jesus promised, even "eternal life."

If I will receive many times more in this life, what does that mean? Does it mean that I will not feel the loss of home and family that I have left? I believe that if I don't feel the loss I should check for a heartbeat. Should I even be asking whether or not I am doing it "for the sake of the kingdom?" If I am a pastor or worship leader or feeding the poor, no matter what I am doing, am I doing it "for the sake of the kingdom," or would it be better to ask if I am doing it for the sake of the King?

If I won't trust enough to tithe, how am I ever going to get to the standard of forsaking all for the Kingdom. I should ask myself do I really have a King, or am I my own King?

How will I obey the "sell all that you possess and distribute it to the poor?" If I won't kill the sacred cow to save children I should ask the Lord, "Good Teacher, what shall I do to inherit eternal life?"

Do we really believe that this young ruler is the only guy who has to live this standard? Was Jesus using this question to give all of us a life lesson in how to inherit eternal life?

His answer was the same as His calling "come and follow Me."

Chapter 31

CHASING TURKEYS

You know it is hard to soar like an eagle when you are too busy chasing turkeys. At The Father's House Church we have a philosophy about leadership that is very simple. You must follow Jesus first and foremost. Then you must follow the leadership of the church and be teachable. Also, you must be willing to accept the call to be someone that others could follow. This very simple idea brings with it a lifestyle of habit that usually brings all of us to the decision on a daily basis to do the next right thing. When someone is following, we encourage them to watch us to see what we do right and imitate us. We truly are the epistles written on our hearts for all men to see

Jesus said *"It is inevitable that stumbling blocks come, but woe to him through whom they come! It would be better for him if a millstone were hung around his neck and he were thrown into the sea, than that he would cause one of these little ones to stumble."* To cause one to stumble is the same word for the bait used to lure one's prey into a trap. We could end up being bait if we take the wrong turn and then they take the wrong turn.

As leaders of The Father's House we attend church services and respond to our responsibility as an effort to answer the call of Jesus to "follow Me." Jesus said that you could see who loves Him by who it is that obeys Him. As leaders that others are following, we need to consider the life and death outcome that our actions cause when we tell people to imitate us.

Recently, my son-in-law and another leader that I had promoted and ordained were standing at the back of the church when they saw a group of turkeys go walking by. They were amazed to see twenty or so wild turkeys right outside the church door. For some reason that neither of them can explain they took off after these turkeys. They almost caught one when it would get away. Then their adrenaline surged and they continued the chase. They ran over hill and dale chasing these turkeys with all they had (which was not much, they were bare handed). I had asked people where these two had gone and nobody wanted to answer me, this caused me to be suspicious. All of a sudden one of them looked up at the other and asked "what time is it?" "Oh no, it's eleven thirty, we are in trouble." When they got back I asked where they had been? I thought that their explanation was not a very good example to the youth and children that they led. I assigned a essay on the sermon of that day and gave a copy of the day's sermon to them to use in the writing of it.

Louie, my son-in-law, wrote a story telling of his life. His was a life of no leadership. A life that eventually became dysfunctional because he had to figure it out as he went. As he came in contact with leadership in school he did not know how to follow. It was other leaderless kids that were influencing him. Obviously, doing it his way became the anthem of his life. Louie, making himself his own leader was going to come face to face with someone who would tell him "you're going the wrong way." That eventually happened with law enforcement and judicial authorities who eventually punished him for every wrong move that he got caught in. They strip searched and confined and punished him. They watched, controlled and required of him things that he did not want to do. All in the name of helping him in ways that he does not want help in. His essay covered all of this and told of his examples of love in his life that were unfair, unfortunate and unloving, except that as a boy he did not know that these were not how it was supposed to be. Then he was brought to The Father's House and Life Recovery Ministry, where he struggles again, with people who are trying to control him.

One day he realized that he cannot succeed here doing what he always did. He is doing what does not work. Here at LRM he has people like Andy Engler from Kalamazoo, Michigan who has come to Oroville to give his life away to be used "for the sake of the Kingdom," and is here to help him. He has Nicole Orsillo my daughter, (who is now his wife) and Steve Orsillo, Danny Harp and a host of others all here to give their lives away for those born in unfair circumstances, and for those who are lost. All here for him, how would he replace that? What do they want him to do? Just follow them! That is all he would be told. Where are they going he would ask? To heaven eventually, but they would teach him how to have eternal life and life abundantly. What is that life abundant he would ask? It is a life that is to receive "many times as much at this time and in the age to come, eternal life." Louie had to come to the difficult decision to quit following his own leadership and doing what he wanted to do and start following someone who had something better than he had. He chose to follow. He has proven to be a good follower and that has caused him to become a good leader.

Recently, Louie asked me how does he become ordained as a Pastor in The Father's House Church? I answered that one of the first requirements was to attend the International Leaders School of Ministry at Toronto Airport Christian Fellowship in Toronto, Canada. He went and his world was turned upside down as he was baptized in the Father's love for him and he found that his value was in God's love for him and his love for God. He understood the privilege of being used by God to lead others to the Father. Not the strip searching, punishing, jailing authority he had always known but the loving Father who created all things for Louie's pleasure and well being. Louie found out that the standards or rules that He required were for Louie's salvation and abundant joy, not to mention Louie's usefulness in leading others to that revelation of the Father's love. It was not to control him or tie him down.

Chasing turkeys was a very revealing essay to me and to Louie, as we both found out so much about who he is as a follower of Jesus and a leader who others are following. If he wants them to fly like eagles like he has, he will have to remember that it is hard to soar with the eagles when you're chasing turkeys! We learned that it is easy to get distracted by all the turkeys walking by.

People come into our lives to bait us into running after things which do not lead to eternal life, distracting us from the job of being someone who, if followed, will lead others towards eternal life. They bait us into making prosperity or security the focus of our lives instead of making the command of Christ to "love one another as I have loved you" the focus. They cause us to seek signs and wonders instead of the instruction of Jesus to "seek first the Kingdom of God," letting the signs and wonders follow us. They want us to read a Proverb a day instead of encouraging us to do the things that will result in the "many times as much at this time" reward and the eternal life that Jesus promised if we live for the "for the sake of the Kingdom of God."

Our enemies come with half-truths just like in the garden with Eve quoting God with words like "did He not say," or attempting to deceive us just like with Jesus in the wilderness. Trying to get our attention onto things that do not give us the eternal life and abundant results that Jesus came to give. Jesus gives it to those who "follow Him."

Following Him does not always look like we think or like people say it should look. I have listened to so many voices in my life. I have followed so many bunny trails in the wrong direction. I have chased so many turkeys.

I have decided to "follow Jesus," no turning back. I have found that the "foxes have holes and the birds of the air have nests but the Son of Man has nowhere to lay His head." I have learned that He wants me to leave all and "follow Him." The Father has given me clear instruction that when faced with the presence of the Law and the Prophets, I should "listen to Him," Jesus is the Him that I should listen to, He is the Father's son.

He would have me "love those who persecute me" and "forgive those who have sinned against me." Turn the other cheek to those who strike me.

Jesus would have me feed the hungry that I see and clothe the naked that I see. He would have me invite the strangers in and visit the imprisoned as if it were He that was a stranger or prisoner. If I would "follow Him" I would preach the good news of salvation and I would "preach the Kingdom."

As the sign that I am one of His I would "lay hands on the sick and they would recover." I would do the things that Jesus did and even greater things would I do. This is the description of what the abundant life is that Jesus described. I would have "love, joy, peace, patience, kindness, goodness, faithfulness, gentleness, and self-control."

I would not participate in these *"the deeds of the flesh are evident, which are: immorality, impurity, sensuality, idolatry, sorcery, enmities, strife, jealousy, outbursts of anger, disputes, dissensions, factions, envying, drunkenness, carousing, and things like these."* If I would follow Jesus these fruit of the flesh would not be evident, I will not carry out the desire of the flesh.

I must not be carried away by the chasing of turkeys. I must be consumed by the love of my Father in heaven and the teachings and example of Jesus.

We are sometimes still carried away with chasing turkeys and we do lose sight of the goal. The goal of becoming like Christ, being transformed into His image. Representing Him, doing what He did and saying what He is saying. Living our lives "for the sake of the Kingdom of God." I will double my effort to understand what is important and what gives life to those who are following me. I will again drop my nets and leave all behind for the sake of knowing Him. For the "sake of the Kingdom," for the sake of the King.

Chapter 32

PAUL

PAUL WAS not always Paul. His name was Saul of Tarsus and he described himself as the Pharisee of Pharisees. He sought out Christians to arrest and would bring them back to Jerusalem bound. He then met Jesus and the rest, they say, is history.

THE CONVERSION OF SAUL

"Now Saul, still breathing threats and murder against the disciples of the Lord, went to the high priest, and asked for letters from him to the synagogues at Damascus, so that if he found any belonging to the Way, both men and women, he might bring them bound to Jerusalem."

"As he was traveling, it happened that he was approaching Damascus, and suddenly a light from heaven flashed around him; and he fell to the ground and heard a voice saying to him, "Saul, Saul, why are you persecuting Me?" And he said, "Who are You, Lord?" And He said, "I am Jesus whom you are persecuting, but get up and enter the city, and it will be told you what you must do."

Jesus said that Saul was persecuting Him when the story says that he was persecuting the saints. We really don't get this idea very well that to feed the poor is to feed Jesus and to persecute each other is to persecute Jesus. This should probably be the focus of our search for the truth for the rest of our lives "following Him." We become Jesus on the earth. When we heal, Jesus is healing, when we feed, Jesus is feeding and being fed. When we come in His name it is as Him, to save, heal, and deliver those who are lost. If we have Christ in us then we have the King in us therefore we have the Kingdom of God in us. When our message is received or we rebuke a demon, the Lord instructs us to tell them that the Kingdom has come near to them this day. Also, when they don't hear our message and they don't get set free, Jesus says that we should tell them that the Kingdom has come near them this day. The Kingdom does not always heal, it is in us and even though it is in us, people must still believe to receive. Jesus said constantly to almost everyone that *"your faith has made you well."* The doing of the healing and the preaching of the Kingdom is not for the sake of the receiver or the preacher, It is for the "sake of the Kingdom." This is what Jesus promised, whatever we do "for the sake of the Kingdom," we will be rewarded many times over in this life and in the next.

Lets get back to the story of Saul as he is born again and made into a "new creature in Christ Jesus."

"The men who traveled with him stood speechless, hearing the voice but seeing no one. Saul got up from the ground, and though his eyes were open, he could see nothing; and leading him by the hand, they brought him into Damascus. And he was three days without sight, and neither ate nor drank."

"Now there was a disciple at Damascus named Ananias; and the Lord said to him in a vision, "Ananias." And he said, "Here I am, Lord." And the Lord said to him, "Get up and go to the street called Straight, and inquire at the house of Judas for a man from Tarsus named Saul, for he is praying, and he has seen in a vision a man named Ananias come in and lay his hands on him, so that he might

regain his sight." But Ananias answered, Lord, "I have heard from many about this man, how much harm he did to Your saints at Jerusalem; and here he has authority from the chief priests to bind all who call on Your name."

"But the Lord said to him, "Go, for he is a chosen instrument of Mine, to bear My name before the Gentiles and kings and the sons of Israel; for I will show him how much he must suffer for My name's sake." So Ananias departed and entered the house, and after laying his hands on him said, "Brother Saul, the Lord Jesus, who appeared to you on the road by which you were coming, has sent me so that you may regain your sight and be filled with the Holy Spirit." And immediately there fell from his eyes something like scales, and he regained his sight, and he got up and was baptized; and he took food and was strengthened."

SAUL BEGINS TO PREACH CHRIST

"Now for several days he was with the disciples who were at Damascus, and immediately he began to proclaim Jesus in the synagogues, saying, He is the Son of God. All those hearing him continued to be amazed, and were saying, "Is this not he who in Jerusalem destroyed those who called on this name, and who had come here for the purpose of bringing them bound before the chief priests?" But Saul kept increasing in strength and confounding the Jews who lived at Damascus by proving that this Jesus is the Christ."

"When many days had elapsed, the Jews plotted together to do away with him, but their plot became known to Saul. They were also watching the gates day and night so that they might put him to death; but his disciples took him by night and let him down through an opening in the wall, lowering him in a large basket."

"When he came to Jerusalem, he was trying to associate with the disciples; but they were all afraid of him, not believing that he was a disciple."

"But Barnabas took hold of him and brought him to the apostles and described to them how he had seen the Lord on the road, and

that He had talked to him, and how at Damascus he had spoken out
boldly in the name of Jesus. And he was with them, moving about
freely in Jerusalem, speaking out boldly in the name of the Lord."

This is quite a story of conversion, going from the persecutor of the
followers of Jesus to becoming a follower, then on to be a preacher
who is persecuted for the "sake of the Kingdom." I don't know how
long it took but the description sounds like a very quick conversion.
Like twenty seconds or so. Then Saul is taken to the known disciples
and taught. He is compelled to tell of his new found knowledge that
Jesus is the Christ.

I don't think any commentary is necessary here, it really speaks for
itself and yet today's Christians don't seem to know this is even possible in the realm of the Kingdom of God. People do change and they
change completely when introduced to the Lord of Heaven and King
of all Kings. He is the Lord Jesus Christ and if He is preached as He
appears here in this story He will change a person's life and they will
go in a different direction. All that He is asking them to do is "follow
Me." If we, as His servants sent to compel the lost would only present
Him in such a way then the lost would find Him. He would heal them
and deliver them. He said in Luke *"For the Son of Man has come to*
seek and to save that which was lost." If we only believed that, we
would see so much more happen in our world and the prayer that we
pray: "Your kingdom come, Your will be done, On earth as it is in
heaven" would be seen every day and our search to find the Kingdom
of Heaven would be over. We would see it every day as people meet
Jesus and they change as Saul changed. Having experienced the Heart
of God in the revelation of Jesus we would then begin to preach the
Kingdom and lay hands on the sick to see them recover. Signs and
wonders would also follow us. The world would know that Jesus is
the Lord, and people would be threatened by the presence of many
disciples. Yes, there would be more stoning and more persecuting going on but the Gospel of Jesus Christ would be remembered in the
way that it is with Saul's conversion.

Then the record says, *"But Saul, who was also known as Paul,"* and we never hear of Saul again. Just like that he is changed and we really begin to see the outcome of being born again, Paul is a replica of Jesus. What does a Jesus replica look like? I believe he looks like Paul.

Here are a few things about Paul the Apostle of Jesus Christ, from Paul himself.

"Paul, a bond-servant of Christ Jesus, called as an apostle, set apart for the gospel of God."

Paul said, *"For to me, to live is Christ and to die is gain. But if I am to live on in the flesh, this will mean fruitful labor for me; and I do not know which to choose. But I am hard-pressed from both directions, having the desire to depart and be with Christ, for that is very much better; yet to remain on in the flesh is more necessary for your sake. Convinced of this, I know that I will remain and continue with you all for your progress and joy in the faith, so that your proud confidence in me may abound in Christ Jesus through my coming to you again."*

"Only conduct yourselves in a manner worthy of the gospel of Christ, so that whether I come and see you or remain absent, I will hear of you that you are standing firm in one spirit, with one mind striving together for the faith of the gospel."

People don't talk like this anymore!

Paul also said; *"but one thing I do: forgetting what lies behind and reaching forward to what lies ahead, I press on toward the goal for the prize of the upward call of God in Christ Jesus. Brethren, join in following my example,* (follow me) *and observe* (examine the fruit) *those who walk according to the pattern you have in us."* (follow them.)

"But whatever things were gain to me, those things I have counted as loss for the sake of Christ. More than that, I count all things to be loss in view of the surpassing value of knowing Christ Jesus my Lord, for whom I have suffered the loss of all things, and count them

but rubbish so that I may gain Christ, and may be found in Him, not having a righteousness of my own derived from the Law, but that which is through faith in Christ, the righteousness which comes from God on the basis of faith, that I may know Him and the power of His resurrection and the fellowship of His sufferings, being conformed to His death; in order that I may attain to the resurrection from the dead."

People don't preach like this anymore!

"And this I pray, that your love may abound still more and more in real knowledge and all discernment, so that you may approve the things that are excellent, in order to be sincere and blameless until the day of Christ: having been filled with the fruit of righteousness which comes through Jesus Christ, to the glory and praise of God."

People don't pray like this anymore!

These are just random excerpts from the letters that our beloved brother has written to us. He said that to "live is Christ" as he pursued the revelation of what it meant to "know the fellowship of His sufferings."

He did eventually die and his dying was to his "gain." He died in a dirt hole of a prison so foul that the guards would not go down there but they would let the Christians go down to bring food and water and serve him in various ways. This allowed Paul to smuggle some of these letters out to us. He rejoiced at this circumstance and wrote about the increase in his faith because of these conditions. He was beheaded in this prison and gained what he had hoped for, he departed to be with Jesus, fulfilling the promise of the Lord to him that he would one day be absent from the body and be present with the Lord.

If you study the teachings of Paul you will find a man who is fully committed to the loving of the Lord Jesus Christ and that he also considers his works to be the evidence of that love.

He invited us as his brethren to *"join in following my example, and observe those who walk according to the pattern you have in us."* He wanted us to follow his example and observe those who are the example.

A study of Paul's life would be absolutely relevant to anyone who would answer the call to imitate him. You would see the religious fervor and righteous anger and even violent response of a true believer as you study. You may even relate and think you are a lot like him, you may see the diligent student and the Pharisee among Pharisees he was. Relating to him when his name was Saul might be easier than relating to him later, as he is born again and even given a new name. You shall be called Paul from now on. This man who uses all of the same zeal and fervor as the man he used to be, uses it for a different purpose now. You will hear him celebrate who he was and mourn how he used it. He is proud of how he used his personality to suffer for Jesus and be the chief among the Apostles as he has to defend his right to be in this fraternity. Listing his qualifications as the one hundred forty five lashes with the whip that he took, the stoning and shipwrecks. Being chased out of town and generally despised for his defense of the Gospel of Jesus the Christ. These are his qualifications according to his written words. He healed the sick, raised the dead, baptized many and had fruitful labor wherever he went. Yet he says this in his letters,

"I count all things to be loss in view of the surpassing value of knowing Christ Jesus my Lord, for whom I have suffered the loss of all things, and count them but rubbish so that I may gain Christ, and may be found in Him, not having a righteousness of my own derived from the Law, but that which is through faith in Christ, the righteousness which comes from God on the basis of faith, that I may know Him and the power of His resurrection and the fellowship of His sufferings, being conformed to His death."

People don't live like this anymore!

I wonder how many of us just can't relate to him, yet he says imitate me as I imitate Jesus. This Paul, the born again one, is just as committed as the Saul of the Law except that what he imitates is no longer the old covenant but instead he now imitates the Lamb of God who has been sent by the Father, whose works testify of who He is. I will follow Paul and *"one thing I do: forgetting what lies behind and reaching forward to what lies ahead, I press on toward the goal for the prize of the upward call of God in Christ Jesus."* Yes Lord and Amen!

Chapter 33

PETER

HOW AWESOME it is to read about these Apostles and we see them recruited by Jesus to "follow me." Then we get to follow along in their
extraordinary lives as they watch and learn from the Master. It is hard
to believe reading these verses that Paul and then Peter, James and
John ever fell short in their understanding of what God would have
for them as they give their lives away for the "sake of the Kingdom"
as Jesus had told them to.

Peter is a most remarkable man and the favorite of many. He is
commended by Jesus in the following conversation; "*He said to them,
"But who do you say that I am?" Simon Peter answered, "You are
the Christ, the Son of the living God." Jesus said to him, "blessed are
you, Simon Barjona, because flesh and blood did not reveal this to
you, but My Father who is in heaven."*

His answer to Jesus' question "who do you say that I am" caused
Jesus to change his name and call him Peter instead of Simon.

Peter answered the question of who he believed Jesus was by declaring, "*You are the Christ, the Son of the living God.*" Because Peter had decided that Jesus was the Christ, Jesus called Peter the rock. Now what this word Peter means is piece of the rock or chip off the rock. In translation, Jesus was saying that Peter was a chip off the old block of the rock. The rock, that is Jesus, the chief cornerstone that the builders would reject. On the Rock of Jesus and the chips of that rock like Peter He will build His church. Which is what He said in the following quote.

"*I also say to you that you are Peter, and upon this rock I will build My church; and the gates of Hades will not overpower it. I will give you the keys of the kingdom of heaven; and whatever you bind on earth shall have been bound in heaven, and whatever you loose on earth shall have been loosed in heaven.*"

That is a lot of power and authority to be given for knowing who Jesus is. This is Peter and this is why he turned out to be who he turned out to be.

We all know of his famous failures like cutting off ears and sinking in the waves, not to mention denying that he even knew Jesus. Yet, it is Peter who Jesus calls a chip off the old rock. Jesus said that Peter was a piece of the rock, the very Rock of our Salvation.

Here are some of the ways that Peter would describe himself, plus a few of the things that He would want you to know about being Christian and following Jesus!

"*Peter, an apostle of Jesus Christ, To those who reside as aliens, scattered throughout Pontus, Galatia, Cappadocia, Asia, and Bithynia, who are chosen according to the foreknowledge of God the Father, by the sanctifying work of the Spirit, to obey Jesus Christ and be sprinkled with His blood: May grace and peace be yours in the fullest measure. Though you have not seen Him, you love Him, and though you do not see Him now, but believe in Him, you greatly rejoice with joy inexpressible and full of glory, obtaining as the outcome of your faith the salvation of your souls.*"

"*Therefore, prepare your minds for action, keep sober in spirit, fix your hope completely on the grace to be brought to you at the revela-*

tion of Jesus Christ."

"As obedient children, do not be conformed to the former lusts which were yours in your ignorance, but like the Holy One who called you, be holy yourselves also in all your behavior; because it is written, YOU SHALL BE HOLY, FOR I AM HOLY."

"If you address as Father the One who impartially judges according to each one's work, conduct yourselves in fear during the time of your stay on earth; knowing that you were not redeemed with perishable things like silver or gold from your futile way of life inherited from your forefathers, but with precious blood, as of a lamb unblemished and spotless, the blood of Christ. For He was foreknown before the foundation of the world, but has appeared in these last times for the sake of you who through Him are believers in God, who raised Him from the dead and (gave Him glory, so that your faith and hope are in God)."

Wow!!! "If you address as Father the One," you should "conduct yourselves in fear." Where is that ever talked about yet it is the Jesus replica Peter who says this, we should listen to what he tells us, he is the disciple and Apostle of the Lord Jesus Christ. This is how he describes himself.

He continues!!

"Therefore, putting aside all malice and all deceit and hypocrisy and envy and all slander, like newborn babies, long for the pure milk of the word, (I think people have left churches because of the milk of the word, ouch!) (could this be what is meant by the saying 'thinking themselves wise they became foolish'?) so that by it you may grow in respect to salvation, if you have tasted the kindness of the Lord. But you are A CHOSEN RACE, A ROYAL PRIESTHOOD, A HOLY NATION, A PEOPLE FOR GOD'S OWN POSSESSION, so that you may proclaim the excellencies of Him who has called you out of darkness into His marvelous light; for you once were NOT A PEOPLE, but now you are THE PEOPLE OF GOD; you had NOT RECEIVED MERCY, but now you have RECEIVED MERCY. Beloved, I urge you as aliens and strangers to abstain from fleshly lusts which

wage war against the soul. Keep your behavior excellent among the Gentiles, so that in the thing in which they slander you as evildoers, they may because of your good deeds, as they observe them, glorify God in the day of a visitation."

If we as the church were to be held up to a mirror would the church reflect these sayings like 'A CHOSEN RACE, A ROYAL PRIEST-HOOD, A HOLY NATION, A PEOPLE FOR GOD'S OWN POSSESSION?' Is this what we would see reflected in the mirror as we answer the call of Jesus and the example of Peter to follow Jesus?

Here is more from Peter, the chip off the Rock.

HONOR AUTHORITY

"Submit yourselves for the Lord's sake to every human institution, whether to a king as the one in authority, or to governors as sent by him for the punishment of evildoers and the praise of those who do right."

"For such is the will of God that by doing right you may silence the ignorance of foolish men. Act as free men, and do not use your freedom as a covering for evil, but use it as bond slaves of God."

"Honor all people, love the brotherhood, fear God, honor the king."

"Servants, be submissive to your masters with all respect, not only to those who are good and gentle, but also to those who are unreasonable. For this finds favor, if for the sake of conscience toward God a person bears up under sorrows when suffering unjustly. For what credit is there if, when you sin and are harshly treated, you endure it with patience? But if when you do what is right and suffer for it you patiently endure it, this finds favor with God."

Wow again!!! These words speak for themselves, I am humbled and challenged by them!! Do we dare continue?

CHRIST IS OUR EXAMPLE

"For you have been called for this purpose, since Christ also suffered for you, leaving you an example for you to follow in His steps, WHO COMMITTED NO SIN, NOR WAS ANY DECEIT FOUND IN

HIS MOUTH; *and while being reviled, He did not revile in return;* *while suffering, He uttered no threats, but kept entrusting Himself* *to Him who judges righteously; and He Himself bore our sins in His* *body on the cross, so that we might die to sin and live to righteous-* *ness; for by His wounds you were healed. For you were continually* *straying like sheep, but now you have returned to the Shepherd and* *Guardian of your souls."*

Big shoes to fill, help us Holy Spirit! Peter says that we should "follow in His steps." Be His replica? Do as He has done. Now how do we appear in the mirror? Like Jesus I hope, that is the world's hope, that is the hope of the lost.

"You have been called for this purpose, since Christ also suffered *for you, leaving you an example for you to follow in His steps."*

Suffer for the world is the example and following in those steps is the challenge. Again, Wow!!!!!!

I am in awe of this man Peter, he failed and knew it. He was even told in advance that he would fail. Then Jesus tells him that when he is old he will have another chance and this time he won't fail.

Peter knew that he would die for the "sake of the Kingdom." Peter did die in the manner described by Jesus. History tells us he was crucified upside down, that he died for the sake of the King.

I will follow you Peter as you "follow Him." I am proud to call you brother and your words are the word of God to me.

Chapter 34

JAMES

MOST COMMENTATORS I have read say that they believe that this James is the brother of Jesus. He is said to have died as a martyr for the "sake of the Kingdom." In the gospels it is clear that Jesus' brothers and family, other than His mother, did not believe that He was the son of God.

Here in the epistle that we have, one that James wrote, it is clear that James does now believe that Jesus is the Savior of all mankind. He says that he is Jesus' servant, slave even. James, in the first line of his letter calls his brother *"the Lord Jesus Christ."* A rather radical change from the record in the gospel.

It is likely that the family saw Jesus crucified. If not, then the legend of that death along with the testimony of their mother would certainly be enough to believe that Jesus did die and He did say from the cross the things He is famous for. Then came the report, He is alive! Raised from the dead. I don't know for certain what caused James to believe in Jesus but he does eventually believe. In the letter that becomes known as the Word of God, one that we call The Book of James, he says some awesome things. Here are some excerpts from these words.

TESTING YOUR FAITH

"James, a bond-servant of God and of the Lord Jesus Christ, to the twelve tribes who are dispersed abroad: Greetings. Consider it all joy, my brethren, when you encounter various trials, knowing that the testing of your faith produces endurance. And let endurance have its perfect result, so that you may be perfect and complete, lacking in nothing. But if any of you lacks wisdom, let him ask of God, who gives to all generously and without reproach, and it will be given to him."

The expectation to *"Consider it all joy, when you encounter various trials"* is a very difficult standard to live. It does not feel like joy when I encounter testing. I will have to be very happy with the result that I receive. When I was young I would work out with weights with the expectation of getting bigger, better looking muscles and I would take my shirt off whenever possible to show them off. I had worked very hard and suffered pain to achieve this result. Thus the saying, 'no pain, no gain,' the pain of working out causes joy when the results are enjoyed.

James says that we should "consider it all joy" because the hardship or "trials" will produce a testing of our faith which produces endurance. I would have to think very highly of endurance to even be okay with hardship, let alone considering it all joy.

Does that mean when I ask the Lord to increase my faith that I am asking Him for trials and hardship?

Then James says, when faith increases it "produces endurance," which will have "its perfect result" and I will be "perfect and complete, lacking in nothing." Really? "Perfect and complete? Lacking in nothing?" I wonder what letting endurance have its result looks like? Is it like when your running long distance and your lungs feel like they are going to explode and every fiber of your being wants you to stop, but you don't?

This would be an incredible outcome to the church if its members were able to "consider it all joy," then continue as the process of endurance has "its perfect result." I think that if one member could do this it would incredibly change the life of a local church. That person would infect the whole congregation and the leaven affecting the whole lump of dough would not be a rotting effect but a completing and perfecting effect.

This one phrase out of a whole epistle, heck out of the whole New Testament, would cause us as lovers of God and bond servants to Jesus, to be perfected and complete. These apostles made bold statements and James made a bold promise here. If you listen to the messages from the pulpits of American churches, you don't get the impression that people are seeking faith by "Hearing the word of God" (the Word that became flesh and dwelt among us) or wanting what faith they have "tested," so it "produces endurance," with the outcome being that endurance can have its "perfect result." A definite outcome is a bold promise, James was a bold man, willing to endure for the "sake of the Kingdom."

James continues

"Blessed is a man who perseveres under trial; for once he has been approved, he will receive the crown of life which the Lord has promised to those who love Him."

"Therefore, putting aside all filthiness and all that remains of wickedness, in humility receive the word implanted, (this is not a book) which is able to save your souls."

"But prove yourselves doers of the word, and not merely hearers who delude themselves."

"For if anyone is a hearer of the word and not a doer, he is like a man who looks at his natural face in a mirror; for once he has looked at himself and gone away, he has immediately forgotten what kind of person he was."

It is so clear that James knew that it was not going to be good enough just to hear the message of Jesus. One would have to then believe with a belief that had actions involved, actions of obedience to the 'Word of God implanted' in their souls.

THE SIN OF PARTIALITY

"My brethren, do not hold your faith in our glorious Lord Jesus Christ with an attitude of personal favoritism. For if a man comes into your assembly with a gold ring and dressed in fine clothes, and there also comes in a poor man in dirty clothes, and you pay special attention to the one who is wearing the fine clothes, and say, you sit here in a good place, and you say to the poor man, you stand over there, or sit down by my footstool, have you not made distinctions among yourselves, and become judges with evil motives? Listen, my beloved brethren: did not God choose the poor of this world to be rich in faith and heirs of the kingdom which He promised to those who love Him?"

"For judgment will be merciless to one who has shown no mercy; mercy triumphs over judgment."

The heading on this paragraph says this is about the sin of partiality. I think it is really about the value we place on riches and the damage money does to our inheritance. We pursue it to the exclusion of our desire to inherit the Kingdom of God. We preach money as the proof of our faith. Is this rich man in the story likely to have what I need to inherit the Kingdom? James says that the poor man is more likely to have it. I pastor a church called The Father's House Church of Oroville and it is filled with people who may not have been to the very bottom of the suffering barrel, but they have seen the bottom from their vantage point. These brothers and sisters have taught me more about the Kingdom of God than anyone else has ever taught me. They cry from the depth of their souls, they hurt out loud, they know that their only hope is in the Word implanted. Many of them are sick of their selfishness and they know that if they are going to get free they will have to do things differently. They will have to do works of unselfishness. They will have to persevere through trials and build an endurance. One that will perfect their faith. Faith that will save them.

FAITH AND WORKS

"*What use is it, my brethren, if someone says he has faith but he has no works? Can that faith save him? If a brother or sister is without clothing and in need of daily food, and one of you says to them, go in peace, be warmed and be filled, and yet you do not give them what is necessary for their body, what use is that? Even so faith, if it has no works, is dead, being by itself. But someone may well say, "you have faith and I have works; show me your faith without the works, and I will show you my faith by my works."*

"You believe that God is one You do well; the demons also believe, and shudder."

"But are you willing to recognize, you foolish fellow that faith without works is useless?"

There is that word useless again. Just like when Jesus said that salt would be useless if it lost its saltiness.

"Was not Abraham our father justified by works when he offered up Isaac his son on the altar? You see that faith was working with his works, and as a result of the works, faith was perfected; and the Scripture was fulfilled which says, 'AND ABRAHAM BELIEVED GOD, AND IT WAS RECKONED TO HIM AS RIGHTEOUS-NESS,' and he was called the friend of God. You see that a man is justified by works and not by faith alone."

"For just as the body without the spirit is dead, so also faith without works is dead."

Could it be more clear, or more easily understood? Where are the works of the church or of Christian believers? There are reportedly one hundred million Christians in the United States. The evidence of these works that should be the demonstration of our faith are not so easily identifiable as you would think that they should be. In every city you find the believers who have heard these words and believed them. Yet the evidence of one hundred million believers just is not there to conclude that we are a nation that believes the words of

James. That "faith without works is dead," or that without works our faith cannot be justified. Since it is impossible to please God without faith and faith is justified by her works then I must conclude that without works it is impossible to please God.

James has come from growing up with Jesus and not wanting to believe who his brother was. All the time hearing the stories of the old testament about his heritage and the promise of the Messiah or Christ that would deliver the people of Israel from their sins. Then James is asked to believe that his own brother Jesus, is that Christ. Here in the opening phrase of his letter to us, James declares that Jesus is Lord and He is the Christ. Men change when they follow Jesus, James has changed and he followed Jesus to his death as he was killed for his faith and will be counted among the martyrs that we read about in The Revelation of Jesus Christ. His words are the Word of God to me and I will give thanks to God our Father and The Lord Jesus Christ for James and I will do as he has said, I will love because I have been loved and I will do works so that my faith can be justified.

Chapter 35

JOHN "THE DISCIPLE THAT JESUS LOVED"

JOHN REFERRED to himself as the disciple that Jesus loved and I think if more of us referred to ourselves with such positive descriptions the world would take on the appearance of being a loved world. During my pre-marital meeting my pastor said "if after twenty years your wife is not all that you want her to be then you have not loved her into it." The idea being that if you love your wife and she knows she is loved, she will become the woman that you need her to be. Both by her changing and by your needs changing to line up with what she has to give. Love causes an adjustment in us when we know we are loved. To know we are the disciple that Jesus loves would have a profound affect on who we are. The search for our identity would become easy as we would grow confident in who He has caused us to be born again as.

I am the disciple that Jesus loves also. This knowledge alone has caused me to be a better man and a better Christian, as I reflect love from God to people in my world with all of my heart, mind, soul and strength. Just as the moon reflects the light of the sun, I reflect the Light of The World into people's lives. This makes me a light as well, a light of His love.

My love for Jesus is seen in my obedience, just as He said that it would be when He said *"he who obeys me, it is him who loves me."*

John started his first epistle with these words: *"What was from the beginning, what we have heard, what we have seen with our eyes, what we have looked at and touched with our hands, concerning the Word of Life-- and the life was manifested, and we have seen and testify and proclaim to you the eternal life, which was with the Father and was manifested to us-- what we have seen and heard we proclaim to you also, so that you too may have fellowship with us; and indeed our fellowship is with the Father, and with His Son Jesus Christ. These things we write, so that our joy may be made complete. This is the message we have heard from Him and announce to you, that God is Light, and in Him there is no darkness at all. If we say that we have fellowship with Him and yet walk in the darkness, we lie and do not practice the truth; but if we walk in the Light as He Himself is in the Light, we have fellowship with one another, and the blood of Jesus His Son cleanses us from all sin. If we say that we have no sin, we are deceiving ourselves and the truth is not in us. If we confess our sins, He is faithful and righteous to forgive us our sins and to cleanse us from all unrighteousness. If we say that we have not sinned, we make Him a liar and His word is not in us."*

This is the first chapter of John's first epistle. He goes on to write lots of important stuff in just seven chapters spanning three epistles. In these letters John calls the saints his children and talks as a father to his offspring. These men considered those who followed them their children and the one who endangered their faith as enemies. John as "the disciple that Jesus loved" endured many hardships, it is said that he was boiled in oil and survived. Then they exiled him to an island where he wrote the Revelation of Jesus Christ. In this book he tells of a vision of being taken to heaven and shown how the Lord would bring about the end. The name of this vision is the most revealing part to me, The Revelation of Jesus Christ. You hardly ever hear these verses preached on and when you do it is sort of ominous. I have always read it as the revealing of Jesus, as its name says. In this book, The Revelation of Jesus Christ, you get to see just who this Jesus is and where following Him will take you.

John is often quoted as individual sound bites yet seldom preached from the context of his first epistle. Reading this epistle would challenge the best of us to look at ourselves, asking God to search our souls and find any thing that would hinder us from knowing Him. Many of us would wonder what we have believed in. What we believe in may not look or sound anything like this!

CHRIST IS OUR ADVOCATE

"My little children, I am writing these things to you so that you may not sin And if anyone sins, we have an Advocate with the Father, Jesus Christ the righteous; and He Himself is the propitiation for our sins; and not for ours only, but also for those of the whole world. By this we know that we have come to know Him, if we keep His commandments. The one who says, I have come to know Him, and does not keep His commandments, is a liar, and the truth is not in him; but whoever keeps His word, in him the love of God has truly been perfected. By this we know that we are in Him: the one who says he abides in Him ought himself to walk in the same manner as He walked."

Any comment would just take away from His words here. John is the son of a fishermen named Zebedee. He was fishing when Jesus called him to "follow Me," and John did just that. John walked with Jesus and then taught others including me what walking looks like. John says here it can not be faked. The fruit of walking with Jesus is evident in the obedience to the command of Jesus to "love one another as I have loved you." Then John adds a most revealing word, *"one who says he abides in Him ought himself to walk in the same manner as He walked."* John knows that to follow Jesus is to walk in the same manner as He walked. Christianity today with its millions of believers who say they abide in Him, would then have millions of little Jesus', or little Christs as the word Christian literally means. Then the words of Jesus, *"by this all men will know that you are my disciples, that you love one another"* will be evident in the world just as Jesus said that it would be. Then we can each say, I abide in Him.

Do not love the world

"Do not love the world nor the things in the world, If anyone loves the world, the love of the Father is not in him. For all that is in the world, the lust of the flesh and the lust of the eyes and the boastful pride of life, is not from the Father, but is from the world. The world is passing away, and also its lusts; but the one who does the will of God lives forever. This is the promise which He Himself made to us: eternal life."

Wow, John, there really is too much to handle in one sitting here. I will just have to spend the rest of my life digesting these truths and living my life "in order that I may attain to the resurrection from the dead."

Children of God love one another

"See how great a love the Father has bestowed on us, that we would be called children of God; and such we are. For this reason the world does not know us, because it did not know Him. Beloved, now we are children of God, and it has not appeared as yet what we will be. We know that when He appears, we will be like Him, because we will see Him just as He is. And everyone who has this hope fixed on Him purifies himself, just as He is pure. Everyone who practices sin also practices lawlessness; and sin is lawlessness. You know that He appeared in order to take away sins; and in Him there is no sin. No one who abides in Him sins; no one who sins has seen Him or knows Him."

Again, if you did not know that they were fishermen and tax collectors you would have to ask, where did these guys come from and where did they learn to preach like this? The answer, "following Him."

"*Do not be surprised, brethren, if the world hates you. We know that we have passed out of death into life, because we love the brethren. He who does not love abides in death. Everyone who hates his brother is a murderer; and you know that no murderer has eternal life abiding in him. We know love by this, that He laid down His life for us; and we ought to lay down our lives for the brethren. But whoever has the world's goods, and sees his brother in need and closes his heart against him, how does the love of God abide in him? Little children, let us not love with word or with tongue, but in deed and truth.*"

THE COMMANDS OF CHRIST

"*This is His commandment, that we believe in the name of His Son Jesus Christ, and love one another, just as He commanded us. The one who keeps His commandments abides in Him, and He in him.*"

Just believe in Him and Love like He loved you, that's it?

GOD IS LOVE

"*Beloved, let us love one another, for love is from God; and everyone who loves is born of God and knows God. The one who does not love does not know God, for God is love. By this the love of God was manifested in us, that God has sent His only begotten Son into the world so that we might live through Him. In this is love, not that we loved God, but that He loved us and sent His Son to be the propitiation for our sins. Beloved, if God so loved us, we also ought to love one another. No one has seen God at any time; if we love one another, God abides in us, and His love is perfected in us. (That is how they will see Him). By this we know that we abide in Him and He in us, because He has given us of His Spirit. We have seen and testify that the Father has sent the Son to be the Savior of the world.*"

I believe as I read these words to try and find the essence of a man, this man John that is, I am "born again," again. I am convicted and inspired, proud of my commitment and in some ways ashamed. I do know that here in these verses, when I don't try to explain them away to fit my own personal agenda or hide my deficiencies, I am inspired to be a better man. I am inspired to be a more grateful son to my Father in Heaven. I am excited to try again to imitate the "walk in the light" example of my brother John.

John, I will follow you and I will call the words that you wrote the Word of God. I will try with all of my heart to reflect the example of what a man should look like who answers the call of Jesus to "follow Me." The call that you answered. I will hold your life up before me as the reflection of Jesus that I should look like. I too will call myself 'the disciple that Jesus loves."

Chapter 36

JUST AS HE HAD TOLD THEM

HOW DOES the Lord choose His disciples? Jesus practiced a very interesting recruiting policy. He walks up to fellas fishing or collecting taxes and He says "follow Me" and that is it. They either do or they don't.

In this book we have followed along and watched first as twelve were called. We looked at what this life of following could look like and then the words of those who first followed, Peter and John. Then we looked at Paul who is met by Jesus and also called, then James who knew Him all of his life and believed by the evidence that he saw.

We can see their example and the example of so many who live today, it is the fruit of knowing Jesus.

I have shared my reflections of what I have learned through the many years since I first dropped my nets to "follow Him." I have been brought to the point where I understand that I am called of God to imitate Jesus and submit to men. All for the purpose of growing into a little Christ. I have been commissioned to turn to those who have begun the same journey that I have begun and say to them "follow me as I follow Christ," I will lead you to Him. I will show you the way in which we should live. Mostly I would encourage you to hear His voice and, like the sheep, know it is His voice calling you.

Listen to the teachings of the men who have walked with Jesus in the flesh and wrote to tell us what all of this should look like.

I've listened to the teachings of these Apostles and I am a better man because of this. I have loved more, I have given more of what I have received because of their examples. It is hard to believe these are the same guys who fell asleep in the garden and deserted Him at the cross. They wanted to call down fire to consume people and stop a blind guy from getting to Jesus. They went out to change the culture of the world. They did it too. Read their words in the epistles or their history in other writings and see how answering the call to follow Jesus changed them.

To answer His call has changed me. I have been enriched and blessed beyond my ability to express. My life has been so full, as I'm given more and more responsibility in people's lives, as they "follow me."

My wife, my children, my ministries I have been involved in, have been way above my pay grade. I married above my station in life, I served above my ability and have been trusted with way more than I could ever handle on my own or that my training would allow.

It is like the ten servants in the Gospels who were given ten minas. They each got one and when the master returns , the guy who did well and made ten more was not told well done now enter into my rest. He was given ten cities to be in charge of. When you do it right you get more to do. This has proven true in our lives and we love it. Abundant life should not be feared but enjoyed instead. I have enjoyed immensely this abundance that God has called me to. All I did was answer the call of Jesus to "follow Me."

Clearly, we as Christians must "listen to Him," Jesus that is, and learn from Him. His words are not the same teaching as the Law and the Prophets and He does have a standard for who can and "cannot be My disciple."

The words of Jesus will determine whether we are counted among those who are saved by the grace of God or will be judged by whether or not we have obeyed the Ten Commandments. If no other message from this book is implanted in your soul, then please get this one message.

The Father of Heaven and the Creator of all living things has said on several occasions that Jesus is His son. When the Apostles were with Jesus, the Lawgiver Moses, and the Prophet Elijah, the Father spoke out of the mist and said "this is my son, listen to Him." When all of the messages from God and about God, all the messages about how we should follow or how we should look as His people are collected, it is the truth that must prevail. WE SHOULD LISTEN TO THE INSTRUCTIONS OF THE FATHER AND LISTEN TO JESUS.

When the instruction manuals are written on what a Christian should look like, when all of the words are finished being written and read, we should be able to see, if we hold our lives up to a mirror, just exactly what we reflect. We should be able to see what we believe by what we have done, by what we see in the accomplishments of our lives. The answer to the questions should be answered and the most important question would be, do we as the church believe Jesus and His words?

These men, the Apostles bring me to tears as I see their beliefs reflected from their lives and their letters.

We should never forget this simple lesson found in the story of the donkey or the triumphal entry where Jesus gives His disciples the following instructions: "*He sent two of the disciples, saying, Go into the village ahead of you; there, as you enter, you will find a colt tied on which no one yet has ever sat; untie it and bring it here. If anyone asks you, Why are you untying it? You shall say, The Lord has need of it. So those who were sent away and found it just as He had told them.*"

In the life of being Christian I have found that it is always "just as

He had told them." I don't care if Jesus is talking about forgiveness or money, it is going to be, "just as He had told them." If He says how He is coming in the clouds, preparing a place for us, that signs and wonders would follow us or if we believe then all things are possible, I am here to tell you that it will be "just as He had told them." Jesus says that He *"goes to prepare a place for us, that He will send us another comforter, and when the Holy Spirit comes upon us we will receive power from on high."* I know that just as it was with the donkey, it will be "just as He had told them" that it would be.

He said, *"Behold I make all things new, the Son of Man has come to save that which was lost. Today you will be with Me in Paradise. Give and it shall be given to you,"* and I know that it will be "just as He had told them." He will cause rivers of living water to flow from you, you will lay hands on the sick and they will recover, preach the good news to the poor, and my personal favorite, Jesus and His Father will make their homes in me. He said all of this and I am here to say it will be "just as He had told them."

The sheep and the goats will be separated and they will be separated based on what they have done with "the least of these my brethren." "Eternal life" and "eternal punishment" will be the outcome of Him separating us as sheep and goats, "just as He had told them." These very extreme outcomes will be based on what we have done, "just as He had told them."

I cannot vouch for whether it will be as Solomon described it or as any one else promised that it would be. Yet I know that I have obeyed the Father and I "listen to Him," In listening to Him I have heard Jesus proclaim that to be His disciple I must love Him more than all, forsake all possession for "the sake of the Kingdom, pick up my cross and follow Him," feed, clothe, visit and invite the least of these in. Even if Angels themselves appear before me and tell me a different story, I know that it will be "just as He had told them."

As a man who has answered the call of Jesus to "follow Me" I can say this, *"What was from the beginning, what I have heard, what I have seen with my eyes, what I have looked at and touched with My hands, concerning the Word of Life-- and the life was manifested, and I have seen and testify and proclaim to you the eternal life, (Jesus) which was with the Father and was manifested to me-- what I have seen and heard I proclaim to you also, so that you too may have fellowship with me; and indeed my fellowship is with the Father, and with His Son Jesus Christ. These things I write, so that Your joy may be made complete."*

Yes, the Apostle's words are my words too, his testimony is my testimony. I am an eyewitness to the fact that as He has said it would be, it will be just as Jesus "told them." We should take heed to what Jesus said and then to what we do. He said "you will know the Truth and the Truth will set you free"; He said, "He whom the son sets free is free indeed," and it will be "just as He had told them."

Jesus told the disciples that He was going to prepare a place for them in His Father's House. He said *"Do not let your heart be troubled; believe in God, believe also in Me. In My Father's house are many dwelling places; if it were not so, I would have told you; for I go to prepare a place for you. If I go and prepare a place for you, I will come again and receive you to Myself, that where I am, there you may be also. And you know the way where I am going."* Thomas said to Him, *"Lord, we do not know where You are going, how do we know the way?"* Jesus said to him, *"I am the way, and the truth, and the life; no one comes to the Father but through Me."* Jesus said that He is the way to heaven, He is the way to the Father, He is the truth and He is the life, this truth would set us free, why would we follow the words or teachings of any other?

To the Laodiceans Jesus said, *"I know your deeds, that you are neither cold nor hot; I wish that you were cold or hot. So because you are lukewarm, and neither hot nor cold, I will spit you out of My mouth."* Not very comfortable words but we who call ourselves Christian would do well not to ignore these words because it will turn out to be "just as He had told them" that it would be.

If you trust in any other testimony, any other commands, do any other assignments than the ones that you hear Jesus saying as you answer His call to "follow Me," you may not find that the situation is just as you thought that it would be. If you do hear the Father's instructions and you do "listen to Him" as the only voice that you hear in the working out of your salvation with fear and trembling, you will find that it is true, it will be "just as He had told them" it would be.

These fishermen and tax collectors were told by Jesus that if they would "follow Me," He would make them fishers of men. As I have said, they have reeled me in as a fisherman reels in a fish and I love these Apostles of Jesus and I am so grateful for what they have taught me in the lessons of life that comes to anyone who answers the call of the Lord to come "follow Me."

My testimony is that He chased me to an altar where I found out that He was real and in a twenty second prayer I met Him. I said if you're real I will follow you, He was, and I have followed for over thirty four years and counting. I have no regrets and many testimonies of the blessed life that I have had as one who has answered His call. Jesus is and has always remained the Way, Truth and Life for me. If you need help finding Him, I would suggest you call me and I would be happy to show you the way to Him. It really only takes seconds to surrender to His love. Its not very complicated He just says to you, "follow me."

KINGDOM AWAKENING APPRENTICESHIP

KINGDOM AWAKENING APPRENTICESHIP is aimed towards individuals who desire to know more about the Living God and expand their expectation of who He is and who they are as sons and daughters of God.

The environment of the apprenticeship is community and discipleship to help students understand their role in the Kingdom of God and how it relates to the world in which they live.

In addition to class time, students serve in a ministry in the church. There, they serve experienced leaders where they are mentored and inspired to reach the church body and surrounding community. We are compelled by the words of Jesus to His disciples: "as my Father has sent me, I am sending you".

We are committed to develop willing people who have the passion to see a generation move towards true love, true hope and true faith.

Kingdom Awakening Apprenticeship begins with a 6-month Core School where students learn the simplicity and importance of the gospel. Students are then promoted to an additional 6-month internship to practically apply what they have learned. There is also opportunity to move on to 2nd and 3rd year internship.

To learn more please visit **www.kingdomawakening.com**, e-mail **kingdomawakening@live.com** or call **1-800-394-1150**.

LIFE RECOVERY MINISTRIES

LIFE RECOVERY MINISTRIES is a 12-month Christian Discipleship home where men and women who suffer from the disease of addiction can be in a safe place, designed to help turn lives and wills over to the care and control of our Lord Jesus Christ.

Our goal is to have alcohol and drug free men and women who have a strong relationship with Jesus Christ, functioning in a positive manner towards their families and society.

If you are interested please call Danny Harp at (530) 534-4704 or (530) 370-5587

Or you can write us at The Father's House Church, 2661 Elgin St, Oroville, Ca 95966

CPSIA information can be obtained at www.ICGtesting.com
Printed in the USA
LVOW10s0329280713

344981LV00001B/3/P